THE CHILKAT RIVER VALLEY

Volume 11, Number 3, 1984
ALASKA GEOGRAPHIC®

The Alaska Geographic Society

To teach many more to better know and use our natural resources

Editor: Penny Rennick
Associate Editor: Kathy Doogan
Designer: Sandra Harner
Cartographer: Jon Hersh

About This Issue:

The Chilkat Valley has long funneled travelers from ports of southeastern Alaska with their link to the world's marine highways through to the expanses of North America's interior. Ancestors of the Tlingits called the valley their home, and for the past century others have settled on the lowlands surrounded by Southeast's mighty mountains. Judy Shuler of Juneau, a communications specialist with several years' experience as a staff and free-lance writer and public speaker, wrote this comprehensive overview of the land of the Chilkat.

We thank the fine photographers whose images share the beauty of Chilkat country, and we are especially grateful to Gil Mull, and to Elisabeth Hakkinen and members of The Chilkat Valley Historical Society for their review of the manuscript.

(The cover) A powerful beak and stern countenance warn intruders from this eagle's territory. A formidable opponent, a mature eagle has a wingspan of six and one-half to eight feet. (Third Eye Photography)

(Previous page) Winter slowly blankets the Chilkat Valley with ice and snow. The Chilkat Indian village of Klukwan spreads out along the river's shore about 20 miles northwest of Haines. (Third Eye Photography)

ALASKA GEOGRAPHIC®, ISSN 0361-1353, is published quarterly by The Alaska Geographic Society, Anchorage, Alaska 99509-6057. Second-class postage paid in Edmonds, Washington 98020-3588. Printed in U.S.A. Copyright© 1984 by The Alaska Geographic Society. All rights reserved. Registered trademark; Alaska Geographic, ISSN 0361-1353; Key title Alaska Geographic.

THE ALASKA GEOGRAPHIC SOCIETY is a nonprofit organization exploring new frontiers of knowledge across the lands of the polar rim, learning how other men and other countries live in their Norths, putting the geography book back in the classroom, exploring new methods of teaching and learning — sharing in the excitement of discovery in man's wonderful new world north of 51°16'.

MEMBERS OF THE SOCIETY RECEIVE *Alaska Geographic®*, a quality magazine which devotes each quarterly issue to monographic in-depth coverage of a northern geographic region or resource-oriented subject.

MEMBERSHIP DUES in The Alaska Geographic Society are $30 per year; $34 to non-U.S. addresses. (Eighty percent of each year's dues is for a one-year subscription to *Alaska Geographic®*.) Order from The Alaska Geographic Society, Box 4-EEE, Anchorage, Alaska 99509-6057; (907) 563-5100.

MATERIAL SOUGHT: The editors of *Alaska Geographic®* seek a wide variety of informative material on the lands north of 51°16' on geographic subjects — anything to do with resources and their uses (with heavy emphasis on quality color photography) — from Alaska, northern Canada, Siberia, Japan — all geographic areas that have a relationship to Alaska in a physical or economic sense. We do not want material done in excessive scientific terminology. A query to the editors is suggested. Payments are made for all material upon publication.

CHANGE OF ADDRESS: The post office does not automatically forward *Alaska Geographic®* when you move. To ensure continous service, notify us six weeks before moving. Send us your new address and zip code (and moving date), your old address and zip code, and if possible send a mailing label from a copy of *Alaska Geographic®*. Send this information to *Alaska Geographic®* Mailing Offices, 130 Second Avenue South, Edmonds, Washington 98020-3588.

MAILING LISTS: We have begun making our members' names and addresses available to carefully screened publications and companies whose products and activities might be of interest to you. If you would prefer not to receive such mailings, please so advise us, and include your mailing label (or your name and address if label is not available).

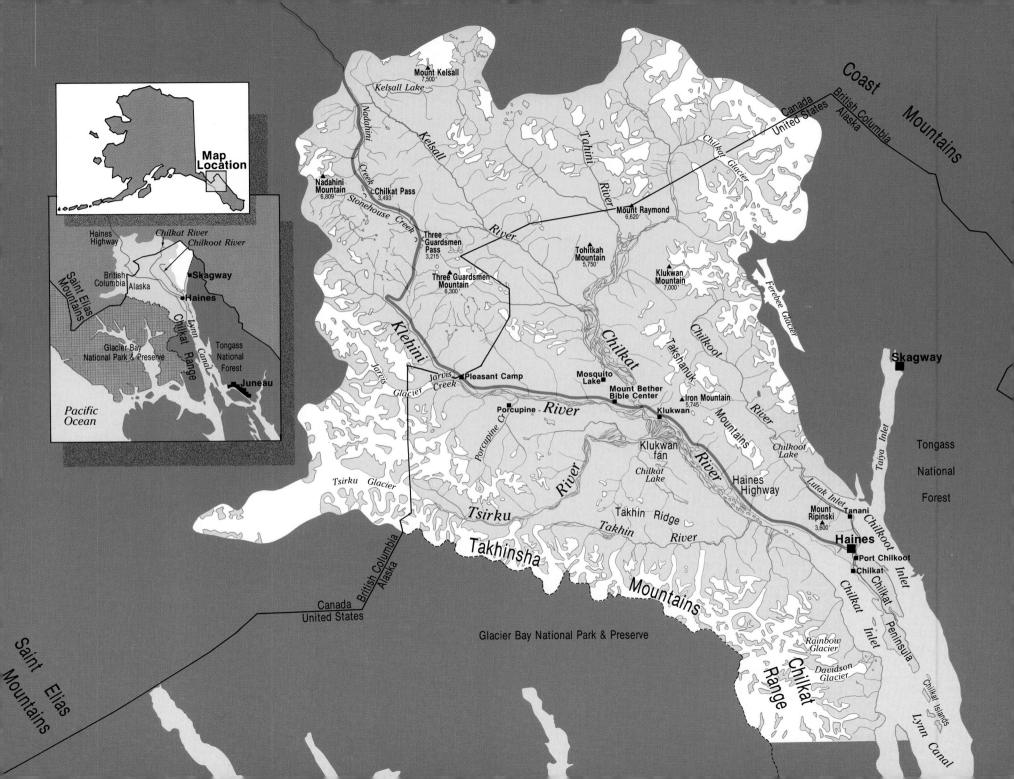

Coast Mountains

British Columbia
Alaska

Canada
United States

Mount Kelsall
7,500'

Kelsall Lake

Nadahini Creek

Kelsall River

Tahini River

Chilkat Glacier

Nadahini Mountain
6,809'

Chilkat Pass
3,493'

Stonehouse Creek

Mount Raymond
6,620'

Three Guardsmen Pass
3,215'

Tohitkah Mountain
5,750'

Klukwan Mountain
7,000'

Three Guardsmen Mountain
6,300'

Ferebee Glacier

Klehini River

Jarvis Creek

Jarvis Glacier

Pleasant Camp

Chilkat

Chilkoot

Takshanuk

Skagway

Mosquito Lake

Mount Bether Bible Center

Iron Mountain
5,745'

Porcupine

Porcupine Cr.

River

Klukwan

Mountains

River

Taiya Inlet

Tongass

National

Forest

Klukwan fan

Chilkat Lake

Chilkoot Lake

Tsirku Glacier

River

Haines Highway

Lutak Inlet

Takhin Ridge

Mount Ripinski
3,600'

Tanani

Tsirku

Takhin River

Haines

Takhinsha

Port Chilkoot

Chilkat

British Columbia
Alaska

Canada
United States

Glacier Bay National Park & Preserve

Mountains

Chilkat Inlet

Chilkat Range

Chilkat Peninsula

Chilkoot Inlet

Saint Elias Mountains

Rainbow Glacier

Davidson Glacier

Chilkat Islands

Lynn Canal

Map Location

Chilkat River
Chilkoot River

Haines Highway

Skagway

Saint Elias Mountains

British Columbia
Alaska

Haines

Chilkat Range

Lynn Canal

Tongass National Forest

Glacier Bay National Park & Preserve

Juneau

Pacific Ocean

Corridor to Canada's Interior

Ensconced in an upper corner of southeastern Alaska, the Chilkat Valley blends climate, flora, and fauna of the coastal rain forest with that of the great interior land mass of Canada's Yukon Territory and a narrow strip of British Columbia.

The transition from a maritime setting to a landlocked one is both rapid and highly visible, making travel through the valley a richly diversified experience. This is the southernmost nesting area for trumpeter swan in Alaska, the northernmost range of the snowberry shrub.

Compared with the remainder of Alaska's panhandle to the south, the Chilkat Valley is drier and sunnier, with warmer summers and colder winters. Yet winters are not so

Glacier-scoured Saint Elias Mountains form a backdrop for the high country along the Haines Highway near the Alaska-Canada border. (Martin Grosnick)

brutally cold as in interior regions of Alaska and Canada.

The Chilkat River system lies as far north as Stockholm, Sweden, draining an area of 958 square miles. Major tributary rivers originate in the glaciers and mountain lakes of British Columbia. They were christened by the Chilkat Indians who for centuries inhabited their banks and traveled their waters. Though the names have evolved through the years, they remain as lyrical in print and on the tongue as the waterways they

From October to February about 3,500 eagles gather along a three- to five-mile stretch of shoreline near the junction of the Chilkat and Tsirku rivers where warm groundwater discharges into the rivers and keeps them ice-free. (Martin Grosnick)

represent. Takhin. Tsirku. Klehini. Kelsall. Tahini. The braided, meandering Chilkat River.

Through the years people have repeatedly traveled to and through this verdant valley which links the lands and waterways of Southeast to

5

mainland Alaska to the west and north. They have come, in turn, as aboriginal inhabitants, as traders, missionaries, prospectors, harvesters of the sea; as soldiers, loggers, hunters, and trappers; as homesteaders, visitors, and recreationists.

Each has brought perceptions of how to use this land and its resources, perceptions which have at times conflicted. Convictions run deep here, where ingenuity and hard work

are prerequisite to economic survival. Communities are small and few in number. Yet in a state which reputedly turns over its population with regularity, it is not uncommon to find Chilkat Valley residents of 15, 20, 25 years and more.

But for many more people this valley has been a corridor. For the Chilkat Indians it provided both a home and a zealously guarded trade route. Gold seekers found it a longer but less rigorous path to Yukon gold than either the Chilkoot or White Pass routes to the east. Contemporary travelers discover in the international route a convenient and incredibly scenic passageway.

The Chilkat Valley still dwells in the shadow of its more celebrated neighbor beyond the Takhinsha Mountains, Glacier Bay National Park and Preserve. Entire histories of Alaska have been written with scant

Loggers show off their skill during the log sawing contest at the Southeast Alaska State Fair in Haines. (Marion Lostrom)

notice of the events or values of the Chilkat Valley. Alaskans themselves are wont to merely pass through en route from here to there. Yet there is much more to warrant a closer look at the history, the resources, the spirit of this place.

Mountains and Sea

Topography of the Chilkat drainage is typical of the coastal terrain of Southeast. Mountains are sculpted to above 5,000 feet, marking the level reached by ice during earlier periods of glaciation. Serrate ridges mark the high divides and glacial cirques are found at valley heads throughout the area.

The Chilkat Range, which lies south of the river valley and separates Lynn Canal from Glacier Bay, is composed of Paleozoic to Middle Mesozoic age rocks. Averaging 4,000 to 5,000 feet, the dominant rock types are Jurassic and Triassic greenstone, schist, graywacke, gneiss, phyllite, and limestone.

At the northern end of the Chilkat Range, clearly visible from the Chilkat Peninsula, Davidson Glacier and Rainbow Glacier are showy remnants of the ice age. When naturalist John Muir explored the area in 1879, he found Davidson Glacier "a broad white flood reaching out two or three miles into the canal with wonderful effect." More than a century later, the glacier has visibly receded. Rainbow Glacier, a few miles north of

Davidson Glacier, is suspended in a high valley about 3,000 feet above sea level.

The glacier-laden Takhinsha Mountains, running east-west with average elevations of 4,000 to 5,000 feet, form a natural boundary between the Chilkat Valley to the north and Glacier Bay to the south. The Saint Elias Mountains lie to the west and the Coast Range to the north of the Chilkat Valley.

Within the valley, the terrane west of the Chilkat River contains abundant metamorphosed Paleozoic igneous rocks, shallow marine sedimentary rocks, and some Cretaceous and Tertiary granitic intrusive rocks.

Geologic interest in the area was kindled by the 1898 discovery of placer gold in Porcupine Creek. After a few decades, recorded geologic study waned until the early 1950s when magnetite deposits were investigated in the Klukwan fan, a gently sloping fan-shaped deposit

Mountains and sea shape the Chilkat Valley and nearby coastline into a curving mass of steep slopes and narrow lowlands, sweeping bays and protruding peninsulas. The Chilkat Peninsula (shown here) reaches south from Haines 11 miles to Lynn Canal. Peaks of the Coast Range rise in the distance, Chilkat Inlet flows at right, and Port Chilkoot, center, is surrounded by forest. (Woody Bausch)

Davidson Glacier flows east of the Chilkat Range to Chilkat Inlet about 10 miles south of Haines. (Shelley Stallings)

where water has deposited debris from nearby higher slopes. Geologic investigations and mapping in the area were performed in 1969-71 by the U.S. Geological Survey.

Most major river valleys in Southeast are structurally controlled by movement of the earth's crust. Major fault zones produce areas of weakness in the rocks, which then are more susceptible to erosion by streams and glaciers.

The Chilkat River Fault is a continuation or major branch of the Chatham Strait Fault, which trends along the major waterway that bisects the Alexander Archipelago. The Chilkat River Fault has never been mapped because it is deeply covered with glacial and stream deposits. However, other faults which trend in the same direction as the Chilkat Fault have been mapped in the valley.

Much of the Chilkat River Valley was scoured by ice to depths greater than 750 feet below sea level. As glaciers retreated, they deposited

Hikers climb on the ice of Le Blondeau Glacier, which extends north from the Takhinsha Mountains to the Tsirku River Valley. (Michael Smith)

debris within the confines of the valleys they carved, either directly from the ice or via streams flowing from glaciers.

The Klukwan fan, a major alluvial fan within the Chilkat drainage, developed at the point where the Tsirku River enters the Chilkat River, near the village of Klukwan. Sand and

gravel deposits lie at least 750 feet thick over bedrock, creating a large aquifer. Groundwater is discharged into the Chilkat River from this aquifer at about 40° F, protecting various sections from winter freezeup.

In midwinter only a single stream drains the fan, losing two-thirds of its water in seepage into the ground before it reaches the Chilkat River. Forty percent of the winter flow in the fan is sustained by groundwater which runs into the Little Salmon River, a major tributary of the Tsirku River. Outflow from Chilkat Lake, and groundwater seeping into Clear Creek at the lake outlet, account for another 50 percent of the total winter flow in the Tsirku River at the head of the fan.

The Chilkat River and its major tributaries drain an area of 958 square

(Above) Fog rises from Chilkat Inlet, an estuary stretching about 16 miles from the mouth of the Chilkat River to Lynn Canal. (Matthew Donohoe)

(Right) A moose stands in the flats of the Chilkat River near its junction with the Takhin. The Takhin Valley is being preserved as prime moose habitat. (George Figdor)

Smoke drifts from a cabin along the Klehini River, a major tributary of the Chilkat, which flows out of British Columbia to join the larger river near Klukwan. (J. Schultz)

The Klehini River gathers its flow from Mineral Mountain (5,124 feet) in British Columbia, 42 miles upstream from its mouth, and from Jarvis Glacier, near the Alaska-British Columbia border 19 miles upstream from the confluence with the Chilkat. Drainage area for the Klehini River is 244 square miles.

Other major tributaries are the Tsirku, Takhin, and Tahini rivers. The Tsirku is fed by glaciers on the north slope of the Takhinsha Mountains, draining 230 square miles along its 25-mile route to the Chilkat River at Klukwan. Six-mile-long Chilkat Lake also flows into the Tsirku River through Clear Creek. Tlingit name for the Tsirku River means "Big Salmon." The Takhin River flows from Takhin Glacier in the Takhinsha Mountains, draining 100 square miles along its 21-mile easterly course to the Chilkat River. Toward the upper reaches of the Chilkat River, near the Canadian border, the Tahini River flows into the Chilkat from its source in Duff Lake, British Columbia.

Just east of the Takshanuk Mountains the Chilkoot River flows 20 miles from near an unnamed glacier in a route roughly parallel to the Chilkat River. Waters gather in 3.6-mile-long Chilkoot Lake before discharging into Lutak Inlet and finally into Chilkoot Inlet and Lynn Canal.

miles, one-quarter of which is covered by ice. The river courses 52 miles from its glacial source in the Coast Mountains of British Columbia to Chilkat Inlet, where it empties silt-laden waters into Lynn Canal.

Longest of its tributaries are the Kelsall and Klehini rivers. The Kelsall River heads in a British Columbia glacier, draining 243 square miles along its 40-mile path to the Chilkat River. The Tlingit name for the Kelsall River was Jelchhini, meaning "Crow River."

14

Rich Earth

Prospectors en route to Klondike goldfields found placer gold about two miles from the mouth of Porcupine Creek in 1898. As news spread, the town of Porcupine sprouted and grew overnight. The following year some one thousand persons were prospecting in Porcupine Creek and nearby streams.

Activity peaked within a few years after initial discovery and then continued only intermittently.

Ravaging floods and the presence of large boulders repeatedly plagued mining operations. An unusually severe flood destroyed principal operations in 1906. In 1908 the Porcupine Mining Company was formed to do large-scale placer mining. The following year the new company constructed a flume more than 1 mile long, 24 to 38 feet wide

Early-day residents of Porcupine stand in front of some of the first tents pitched at the campsite near the junction of Porcupine Creek and the Klehini River northwest of Haines. Prospectors headed for the Klondike discovered gold near the mouth of the creek in 1898. (Yukon Archives, H.C. Barley Collection)

and 6 to 8 feet deep, supported on piles and trestles, to carry the waters of Porcupine Creek past placer ground still to be worked. Construction

PORCUPINE GOLD MINING CO.

Floods repeatedly ravaged placer gold mining operations at Porcupine Creek. In 1909 Porcupine Mining Company constructed a flume one mile long to divert waters of Porcupine Creek past placer deposits still to be mined. (Alaska Historical Library, E.E. Harvey Collection)

(Left) Workers from Porcupine Mining Company build a flume in this view of the company's gold mining operations on Porcupine Creek. Eighty men working in two ten-hour shifts were employed in this large-scale placer operation. (Alaska Historical Library, E.E. Harvey Collection)

(Right) Cables suspended from tepee-shaped trestles carry tubs of earth above the mine workings at Porcupine Creek. (E.E. Harvey Collection, Alaska Historical Library)

17

required more than one million feet of lumber and several thousand piles. This operation continued until August 1915, when another flood filled pits and destroyed the lower part of the flume.

The summer of 1918 was unusually dry at Porcupine. That September torrential rains destroyed much of an elevated flume of even greater dimensions than the flume damaged in 1915.

Between 1898 and 1955, placers in the Porcupine area produced an estimated 60,000 troy ounces of gold.

The U.S. Geological Survey assesses production since 1955 at less than 100 ounces. Recent activity has been limited to small-scale exploration.

The Porcupine Mining District was placed on the National Register of Historic Places in 1976. The town itself no longer exists, and the area is not easily accessible without four-wheel-drive vehicles.

There are perhaps less than a half-dozen operating placer mines in the Porcupine area today, although higher gold prices are renewing interest.

Rusting vehicles and delapidated buildings are all that remain of the town of Porcupine today. Difficult access requiring four-wheel-drive vehicles limits visitors to only the most hardy and determined. (Dave Albert)

One of the active miners is Josephine ("Porcupine Jo") Jurgeleit. The lifelong Haines resident has been working the area 35 years. Each spring she continues to trade her orange-roofed home near town for a tiny three-room cabin at Porcupine, despite amputation of her left leg seven years ago.

Her summer supplies are ferried across the Klehini River by sled in April, while snow is still chest-deep. Later in spring the road to Porcupine is too muddy to support heavy loads. Fuel is hauled in during autumn in preparation for next season's work.

Like most prospectors, Jo Jurgeleit is not inclined to reveal the size of her poke. Whatever the value of the gold that has settled in her sluice box, she talks freely of other compensations:

"I love the outdoors and I love the mining game. I learned geology so I knew what I was doing . . . I feel sorry for people who live in the city and never go out in the woods. There is nothing more peaceful."

It is not hard to understand how Porcupine Creek acquired its name. Jo Jurgeleit says she has spent hundreds of dollars replacing hose eaten by porcupines. She has even had a plate welded under her car to protect engine hoses.

Placer deposits were located mainly near Porcupine Creek and its tributaries and along Glacier, Nugget, and Cottonwood creeks. Smaller deposits were reported on the Klehini River near Jarvis Creek, on Big Boulder Creek, and on upper stretches of the Takhin and Tsirku rivers. Production came almost entirely from Porcupine Creek and its tributaries,

Josephine ("Porcupine Jo") Jurgeleit, lifelong Haines resident shown here weighing gold, has spent more than 35 years searching the Porcupine area for the shiny metal. "I feel sorry for people who live in the city and never go out in the woods," says Jurgeleit. "There is nothing more peaceful." (Judy Shuler)

McKinley and Cahoon creeks. Placers along Glacier Creek and near the mouth of Nugget Creek also account for some production.

Placer gold is generally worn and flattened and ranges from minute

flakes and flour gold to nuggets weighing several ounces. Geologists believe the placer deposits reflect concentrations of gold from nearby lodes.

All known occurrences of lode gold are found in the mountains bounded by the Klehini and Tsirku rivers. Only a few lodes have been staked and exploration is minimal.

Silver, copper, and lead were also reported in a mineralized zone extending across Porcupine, Glacier, and Jarvis creeks south of the Klehini River, but these deposits showed little commercial importance.

While gold was the focus at Porcupine, the Rainy Hollow District at the head of the Klehini River in British Columbia revealed markedly different minerals during the late summer and early fall of 1898. Rainy Hollow minerals were chiefly copper, silver, zinc, and lead, with gold in only negligible amounts. In 1914 about 40 claims were held on several parallel ridges. The area is once again being actively explored.

Primary interest in the Chilkat Valley now centers in a very large deposit of low-grade iron ore at Iron Mountain (5,745 feet), in the Klukwan alluvial fan, and in a similar, but smaller, fan about one mile northwest of the Klukwan fan.

Deposits were originally staked in

A modern-day miner works his placer claim in the Porcupine district. As of early 1983, there were less than a dozen active placer operations in the area. (Dave Albert)

Gold is the treasure at the end of the rainbow for miners along Porcupine Creek. Between 1898 and 1955 an estimated 60,000 troy ounces of gold were extracted from the area. (Dave Albert)

1908, but there was little exploration until after World War II.

Iron is present in the area as a fine-grained magnetite associated with a pyroxenite-type basic rock. Iron and titanium are concentrated in titaniferous magnetite that is widely distributed in the pyroxenite.

Deposits in the fan have eroded from steep canyon walls on Iron Mountain, where the iron-bearing lode deposit outcrops in an area about one mile wide and three miles long. The Klukwan fan contains an estimated 800 million tons of ore averaging 10 percent magnetite.

A study was completed in 1972 to determine feasibility of a strip mining operation that would have a life span of 20 to 25 years, followed by production on underground reserves lasting another 75 years. Although extensive sampling and development work has been completed on the Klukwan fan, there has been little work other than assessment on unpatented claims since 1972.

Barite-rich lodes containing silver and several base metals crop out in rugged glaciated terrain between 3,500 and 5,700 feet near Glacier Creek.

Gold mining accounts for the only real mineral development in the Chilkat Valley to date. The valley's potential for other development continues to attract sporadic interest.

Weather

In general, the Chilkat Valley enjoys weather that is clearer and drier than in other areas of Southeast, with warmer summers and cooler winters. Farther south the transition between seasons often blurs, but here the four seasons are distinct and recognizable.

Even at the southern end of the Chilkat Valley the air is noticeably drier than in other Southeast communities. Average annual precipitation at Haines is 53 inches, compared with 91 inches at Juneau 90 miles south. Skagway, just 15 miles

Fresh snow rides the drooping branches of deciduous trees along the Haines Highway. The Chilkat Valley generally has clearer and drier weather than other areas of Southeast.
(Woody Bausch)

northeast of Haines up Taiya Inlet, is drier still with only 26 inches in average annual precipitation.

Within the Chilkat Valley itself temperature and precipitation can vary markedly as climate moves from coastal to interior.

Weather is monitored at three stations: the small-boat harbor at the foot of Main Street in downtown Haines; near Mile 25 along the Haines Highway at the Klehini River Delta; and at the Canadian customs station at Mile 41 in the Klehini River Valley.

Winter temperatures at the harbor can reach as much as 10° or 15° higher than at the Canadian border. Temperature extremes reflect invasions of air from Canada. The coldest and warmest recorded temperatures in the valley both occurred at Klukwan, Mile 19 Haines Highway: minus 36° F in 1917 and 99° F in 1915. At Haines, the coldest recorded temperature is minus 17° F.

Heaviest snowfalls alternate between

(Left) Fall colors brighten the Chilkat Valley along the Haines Highway. Temperatures and precipitation vary as the region's climate changes from coastal to interior in its sweep up the valley. (Woody Bausch)

(Right) Sizable stands of birch contribute to the Chilkat Valley's brilliant fall colors. (George Figdor)

interior and coast, but snow accumulates to much greater depths in the interior. Near the sea snow more quickly melts or turns to rain. At Mile 10 along the Haines Highway a dividing line often occurs where snow meets rain or precipitation ceases. Through most of America's snowbelt, a rule of thumb says that 10 inches of snow will yield 1 inch of water. With the heavier snows of this region, 4 to 5 inches of snow equal 1 inch of rain.

Strong winds are a regular ingredient of winters throughout Southeast. A high-pressure area commonly centered over interior Alaska in the winter diverts storms to the west or north of the state, or south into the panhandle. Wind speeds may increase drastically as winds funnel through narrow valleys. Strong winds sweep snow from exposed areas, permanently bend trees away from the direction of the prevailing wind, and occasionally keep an entire area free from large trees.

The endless variety of peaks, valleys, ridges, and broad slopes creates different wind patterns and

Mosquito Lake, a popular spot for fishing and relaxation, nestles between the Haines Highway and Chilkat River near Milepost 27. (J. Schultz)

small areas where climate varies. Lutak Inlet northwest of Haines may be completely sheltered from the winds that sweep across its mouth and into Haines from Taiya Inlet.

In summer, sunny, 80° days are not uncommon, making this one of the best places in Southeast to nurture a garden or a suntan.

Forests and Timber Industry

In vegetation, as in climate, the Chilkat Valley is an area of transition.

Two varieties of trees cross the Rocky Mountains westward into the coastal forests at the head of Lynn Canal: lodgepole pine and western paper birch. Subalpine fir appears both here and at the southern end of Southeast. A few species enter Alaska from Canada only at the northeast end of Southeast: Hooker willow, pipsissewa, red mountain-heath, and snowberry.

The dense forest of western hemlock and Sitka spruce is a continuation of a similar forest along the coast of British Columbia, Washington, and Oregon. In the coastal spruce-hemlock forests important conifers are Sitka spruce,

The great forests of Southeast reach into the Chilkat Valley where they are joined by a few interior vegetation species such as lodgepole pine and western paper birch. (John Mackler)

26

western hemlock, mountain hemlock, and Alaska cedar. The lone commercial hardwood is black poplar.

In the Chilkat Valley the spruce-hemlock forest is an overmature, decadent stand. Spruce is declining while hemlock is taking over.

Western hemlock makes up more than 70 percent of the spruce-hemlock coastal forest. It grows well in shallow soils and in shade, reaching heights of 100 or 150 feet. Western hemlock can be identified by long, flat, dark green needles attached in two rows. Cones are only about one inch long, with many tiny, papery scales. The wood is moderately lightweight, moderately hard, with a rather fine and even texture.

Sitka spruce, the state tree, grows largest in Alaska. It can reach to 160 feet with a trunk diameter of 3 to 5 feet. Occasional trees have been found 225 feet tall with trunks more than 8 feet thick. In the Chilkat Valley all conifers tend to be smaller and less dense than in other parts of Southeast.

Unlike the hemlock, Sitka spruce have sharp needles which stand out

Mixed stands of deciduous-coniferous trees cover much of the Chilkat Valley. Black poplar is the only commercial hardwood in the area. (Michael Smith)

Spring growth shoots from the ends of branches of this western hemlock. This species comprises more than 70 percent of the coastal forest of Southeast. (Judy Shuler)

in all directions from the twig. Light orange-brown cones are up to three and one-half inches long. The wood is usually very straight-grained, fine-textured, moderately lightweight, and soft.

Sitka spruce grows mostly in mixed stands with western hemlock, growing more rapidly than the hemlock and requiring more light. Largest trees in old-growth forests may be 500 to 750 years old or more.

Black cottonwood trees grow on flood plains of major rivers and are found extensively along glacial outwash rivers. This species is the largest broadleaf tree in Alaska and northwestern North America, growing rapidly to 80 to 100 feet. On the best sites it can reach 125 feet in 35 years.

A champion black cottonwood, the largest then known, was discovered in 1965 about five miles west of Klukwan. It was growing on a gravel flat 300 feet from the Klehini River.

The stem had broken off many years earlier, but several large branches formed the top. Circumference of the trunk at breast height was 32 feet, 6 inches, and total height was 101 feet. The crown spread an estimated 60 feet. Since then it has completely fallen, probably of old age.

Black cottonwood leaves are shiny dark green above and whitish on the back, with a broad triangular shape and long pointed apex. The tree crosses extensively with balsam poplar where their ranges meet and overlap in the Lynn Canal area. It is difficult to differentiate between the two species, which vary mostly in the seed capsules and flowers.

Among the most important shrubs are willow, copperbush, devil's club, salal, red-osier dogwood, blueberry, huckleberry, highbush cranberry, and snowberry. Red alder is common along streams, beach fringes, and on soils recently disturbed by logging and landslides.

Forests of the Chilkat Valley long provided Tlingits with the raw

Huge black cottonwoods, largest broadleaf tree in Alaska and northwestern North America, grow in river lowlands of the Chilkat Valley. In a little more than three decades of growth, these trees can reach 125 feet in height. (Janet Woodring)

Highbush cranberries, which grow in abundance in the region's forests, are gathered by local residents each fall and used to make sauces, jams, and juices. (George Figdor)

Enticing berries lure unsuspecting pickers into the spines of devil's club. Despite its spiny armament, deer browse on the plant's young shoots. Some Indians hang a sprig of devil's club in their homes to ward off evil spirits. (Judy Shuler)

Sitka spruce grows in a moss-covered forest near Chilkat State Park, south of Haines along Chilkat Inlet. (George Figdor)

material for their houses, canoes, household tools, and carved figures.

Commercial timber harvest started around the turn of the century to meet the needs of two early industries, fish processing and gold mining. Timber stands around Pyramid Harbor were logged to meet the voracious need of canneries for wooden fish boxes. Overharvest of fish soon depleted that resource, however, and the processing industry declined rapidly.

Placer gold mines near Porcupine used lumber for massive flumes. Geologist Henry M. Eakin wrote in 1919 that "the trees are generally of large size, suitable for lumber, and the supply far exceeds any possible demand of the local mining industry. The hemlock is especially adapted for piles and also makes a good grade of lumber. The spruce meets with favor for flume and sluice box lumber, and the cottonwood is preferred for riffle blocks owing to its tough fiber."

Within a few decades gold mining also declined markedly.

Timber harvest would then come into its own as the valley's next major resource industry. At its peak in the mid-1960s through early 1970s, the industry supported two mills and provided perhaps a hundred jobs.

To date about 12,000 acres have been logged in the Chilkat Valley,

Sawdust is burned in a tepee burner at the Schnabel Mill on Lutak Inlet in this 1977 photo. In later years, mill operators did not use the tepee burner. A variety of factors including restricted timber sales and a depressed market has brought hard times to the timber industry around Haines.
(Dave Albert)

A forklift loads timber for export to Japan at Schnabel Lumber Company's sawmill near Haines. (George Figdor)

most of that since statehood. The largest single clear-cutting was harvested on the Kelsall Flats near the Canadian border. Other areas of previous logging activity are located at Mosquito Lake and along the Klehini River.

To buoy up the depressed timber industry, state officials in 1979 signed a contract with the valley's major operator to log timber on state land.

Holder of the contract is Schnabel Lumber Company, a name which has long been synonymous with timber harvest in the Chilkat Valley.

The company began operations at Jones Point, a mile out of town toward the airport, in 1939. During the next few decades the mill expanded, and sold lumber products in Juneau, in Whitehorse, Yukon Territory, and along Alaska's road network.

In 1965 Schnabel sold its mill at Jones Point to Alaska Forest Products and built a new plant at tidewater on Lutak Inlet. Schnabel also purchased and installed a veneer mill and chip production and loading facility here. Timber sales were greatly restricted after 1971. Alaska Forest Products

ceased operation in 1975 and auctioned its plant in 1976. Schnabel Lumber Company was sold in 1983. The state timber contract is still with Schnabel, which has been renamed Pacific Forest Products.

A severely depressed world timber market and remaining timber stands that are less economical to harvest than those in other parts of Southeast have curbed all but very small timber operations in the valley. A handful of small-scale operators currently harvest about 30 acres of timber per year.

One of the best pulpwoods for paper and paperboard, and products such as rayon, western hemlock is also used for general construction, railway ties, mine timbers, and marine piling. The wood is also suited for boxes and crates, interior finish cabinets and flooring, and plywood veneer.

Sitka spruce produces high-grade wood pulp. High-grade lumber from large, clear trunks is important for airplane construction, oars, ladders and scaffolding, boats, and piano sounding boards. Low-grade lumber is made into salmon packing boxes, food containers, shelving, and kitchen furnishings.

Logs await processing at the Schnabel Mill in Haines. (Marion Lostrom)

Wildflowers

Wildflowers bring a flurry of color to the Chilkat Valley and its parks and recreation sites.

One of the earliest to emerge is the showy yellow skunk cabbage. The stately plant inhabits moist, swampy areas, earning its inelegant name through a rather unpleasant odor. It is a favorite with bears emerging from winter dens.

May through July is the peak season for most wildflowers in the Chilkat Valley.

Chilkat State Park on the Chilkat Peninsula south of Haines blooms with the bright yellow tundra rose or cinquefoil; the familiar pink prickly rose; wild flag, a dark blue iris; the aptly named brown chocolate lily; deep pink shooting star; and the graceful red and yellow western columbine. A massive pink rose patch can be seen in the southern portion of the park near the boat launch.

Along the entrance road to Chilkoot Lake Recreation Site, a patch of

One of the earliest plants to bloom in Chilkat Valley, skunk cabbage grows in moist areas and is a favorite of bears coming out of their winter dens. (Woody Bausch)

shooting stars creates a blanket of color.

Berry pickers can gather blueberries, huckleberries, and highbush cranberries along Mud Bay Road in and around Chilkat State Park, at Chilkoot Lake, and around Mosquito Lake. The hiking trail up Mount Ripinski (3,600 feet) is also lined with blueberries. Berries are at their peak from mid-August through September. Other berries available in the region include salmonberry, nagoonberry, cloudberry, wild strawberry, crowberry, wild raspberry, currants, and lowbush cranberry.

Other wildflowers in the Chilkat Valley include the bright yellow western buttercup which grows in coastal alpine areas; the long-stemmed marsh marigold; aquatic common bladderwort; the pale yellow Indian paintbrush; the omnipresent magenta fireweed; the creeping reddish purple beach pea.

Other local flowers are the daisylike fleabane; white-flowered baneberry with poisonous red or white berries; fuzzy cotton grass; the feathery white goatsbeard found in open woods; the bunchberry, a dogwood with white flowers and bright red berries.

Poisonous water hemlock is common in wet meadows, ditches, along streams and along shallow

Colorful wild iris grows in marshy areas throughout the Chilkat Valley. (George Figdor)

Alaska blueberries, endemic to Southeast, attract berry pickers to Chilkat State Park, Chilkoot Lake, and Mosquito Lake. Pink flowers become dark blue-purple berries by late July or August. (Martin Grosnick)

In early summer local residents avidly harvest wild strawberries near Haines. These berries, as well as several domestic varieties, grow exceptionally well in the area.
(George Figdor)

edges of lakes, ponds, and bogs. Growing three and one-half to seven feet high on stout stems, water hemlock has small white flowers in stalked clusters which radiate from the main stalk. When the root is cut lengthwise, it shows many cross-partitioned chambers and a brownish orange, strongly disagreeable substance oozes out. The plant is deadly poisonous and should be known to anyone who eats plants.

Labrador tea, an aromatic shrub with clusters of white flowers, is common in the woods, alpine tundra, and boggy areas. Wild celery or cow parsnip grows an unbrellalike cluster of white flowers 12 to 18 inches in diameter atop hollow, stout stems 6 to 8 feet tall.

Showy spikes of purple blue lupine can be found along dry roadsides. Alaska's state flower, the sky blue forget-me-not, is found throughout the Chilkat Valley.

Among the rare flowers reported in the valley are the blue or lavender *Phacelia sericea;* a small white primrose, *Primula egalikensis;* the stateside mountain lady's slipper; and the mitrewort, *Mitella trifida.*

Purple wild geranium stands out in a field of silverweed. The wild geranium is also known as cranesbill because its seed pod resembles a crane's bill before the pod opens to scatter its seeds. (J. Schultz)

Silverweed (yellow) and cow parsnip color the shoreline of Chilkat Inlet near Haines. (J. Schultz)

Frost rims the edges of dogwood leaves in Chilkat State Park. (Matthew Donohoe)

Wildlife

Because of its transitional setting, the Chilkat drainage harbors one of the most diverse mixes of animal life in Southeast. Moose, mountain goats, bears, wolves, lynx, coyotes, and small furbearers use the various habitats found there.

The valley supports one of the most significant moose populations in the Alaska Panhandle. Chilkat moose tend to be smaller than their counterparts in the remainder of the state. The Haines-Chilkat Range moose herd originated from migrations through the river drainages from Canada in the 1930s. Early roadways may have provided another passageway for the animals. After a population decline in the late 1960s and early 1970s, the herd is currently estimated at 300 to 500.

In October 1981, 20 moose were captured, ear-tagged, and fitted with radio transmitters for aircraft

A cow moose and her calf feed in a pond along the Haines Highway. The Chilkat Valley supports one of the most significant moose populations in Southeast. These largest members of the deer family originally migrated into the area from Canada along river drainages. (Janet Woodring)

monitoring by Alaska Department of Fish and Game biologists. Early observations indicate the moose move seasonally in response to snow depths and available forage. Snow deeper than 35 inches generally restricts their movements. In late winter and early spring, as snow starts to melt, moose appear to move into the forest to feed on emerging green shoots.

The Chilkat Valley hosts a healthy population of mountain goats in all the higher mountain areas. Motorists can see them most easily on Iron Mountain near Klukwan.

The number of goats declined throughout Southeast in the early 1970s, but most populations have rebounded. A firmer estimate of the number of goats in the Chilkat drainage will be developed by state biologists during the next few years.

Mountain goats in the lower Kelsall River drainage were radio-collared in October 1981, and August 1982, to determine their winter use of forest habitat. Like moose, they appear to move under the forest canopy in early spring to eat new vegetation.

Highly sensitive to any disturbance, goats rush to the most precipitous nearby rocks at first sign of harassment. Their habitat must offer routes of escape from harsh weather and from predation by bears, wolves, and wolverines.

Mountain goats inhabit precipices throughout the Chilkat Valley. Iron Mountain, near Klukwan, provides opportunities for viewing these shaggy monarchs of high places.
(Shelley Stallings)

Both black and brown bears are common in the Chilkat Valley, with blacks more numerous than browns. Prime habitat for the black bear is provided by the valley's climax and semi-open mature forest areas with good food-producing understory. Brown bears use a variety of habitats, but generally prefer more open grassland or tundra environments.

Many a valley backyard and garden have hosted bears, even within the city limits of Haines. Sometimes the animals appear more curious than hungry. A cream-colored brownie lingered along a trail, seemingly listening to music and baseball on a transistor radio.

With a rich diet of spawning salmon close at hand, Chilkat brown bears can surpass the size of interior brown bears. Their colors range from blond to dark brown.

Black bears likewise show a wide range of colors. A few instances of glacier or blue bears, a rare color phase of black bears, have been reported in the area. Black bears are easily distinguished from brownies by their straight facial profile and sharply curved claws. The size of black bears is often overestimated, perhaps because of their ability to startle and intimidate. The average adult male black bear weighs about 250 pounds in the fall. By contrast, a brownie male can weigh 500 to 900 pounds before denning.

Wolves are found throughout the Chilkat drainage. There is a high frequency of black wolves, a color phase more common in Southeast than in the Interior. During studies of moose and goat habitat, wolf tracks were often found in moose-feeding areas in the forest, and wolves were seen in the high mountains near small groups of goats.

Although both species are common in the Chilkat Valley, black bears, which usually prefer forested areas, outnumber their larger cousins, the brownies, which generally inhabit more open areas. (Woody Bausch)

A red squirrel, one of the smallest mammals of Chilkat Valley, nibbles on a rose hip.
(Martin Grosnick)

Crafty and adaptable, coyotes, such as this one waiting near the Haines Highway, range throughout the Chilkat Valley as do their larger relatives, wolves. (J. Schultz)

41

Coyote tracks and trails were frequently found in river bottoms near open water and along riverbanks, stream channels, sloughs, and forest edges. Coyotes seem to repeatedly follow the same trails. Lynx have become abundant after a low population for several years. Snowshoe hares, an important source of food for lynx, wolves, and coyotes, are currently widespread in river bottom alder, cottonwood, and willow. Dense stands of brush provide food and protective cover for the hares.

Marten depend on old-growth forest, and their tracks are frequently observed in spruce stands during winter, particularly near the bases of large trees. Muskrats are found in river bottom marshland. The Chilkat Valley is a good area for muskrat compared to the remainder of Southeast, but not when compared to Alaska as a whole.

Big game and furbearing animals in the Chilkat Valley provide family food, sport, and supplemental income.

The upper Chilkat River Valley yielded an unusually high harvest of lynx during the winter of 1983. Red

Sea lions sun themselves at their rookery along Lynn Canal south of Haines. Each spring large numbers of sea lions follow the hooligan runs to the mouths of the Chilkoot and Chilkat rivers. (George Figdor)

Killer whales ply waters of Chilkat Inlet near Haines. These streamlined hunters range worldwide from the Beaufort Sea in the Arctic to Antarctica. (Kurt Ramseyer)

and cross fox were also caught in numbers larger than usual. Other furbearers sought by trappers include wolverine, otter, marten, mink, coyote, and the elusive wolf.

Fur pelts can provide extra cash during lean winter months, but successful trapping requires vast areas and for most it is a marginal vocation. There are perhaps 15 serious trappers in the valley, a number that pretty well saturates the entire area, according to local residents.

For residents of other parts of

Southeast, the Chilkat Valley represents the only place where moose hunters can ride the ferry, then find easy access to moose habitat via the road system. Annual moose harvest averages 25 to 30 per year.

Among the 405 species of birds found in Alaska, about 280 have

(Above) With the longest migration route of any North American bird, arctic terns shuttle from northern latitudes of this continent to southern South America and subantarctic islands between breeding and wintering grounds. Pyramid Island and the northern end of Chilkat Lake support small arctic tern rookeries. (John and Margaret Ibbotson)

(Below) Semipalmated plovers, this one with chicks, nest along tidal zones in the Chilkat Valley. (Mark McDermott)

occurred in Southeast. The Chilkat Valley provides both a migratory route and a wide variety of habitat for year-round and seasonal residents. Bird-watchers traveling through the valley can note the passage from coastal to interior and lowland to alpine areas by the changing bird communities.

The varying habitats include salt water; shorelands along the tidal zone; estuaries and wetlands where flowing fresh water meets tidal areas; freshwater lakes, ponds, bogs, rivers, and streams; woodlands; and alpine areas above timberline.

Spring migration peaks around late April through mid-May. Fall migration is more protracted. Earliest fall migrants, the shorebirds, stop along the tide flats by late August. Passerines, the songbirds, follow in September. October brings the major migration of waterfowl.

Seabirds using saltwater habitat of Lynn Canal and its inlets include gulls and terns. This area lies toward the southern nesting range of the arctic tern, which has the greatest breeding range of any Alaskan water bird. Breeding terns have been recorded as far north as Barrow, as far south as Tracy Arm 120 miles south of Haines. There are small arctic tern rookeries on Pyramid Island and at the northern end of Chilkat Lake.

Abundant winter residents in bays and channels include Barrow's goldeneye, oldsquaw, white-winged scoter, and surf scoter. Breeding birds move to freshwater lakes and streams in southcentral and interior Alaska in spring, while nonbreeders may stay year-round in Southeast.

Among the birds using shorelands along the tidal zone as primary habitat are the greater yellowlegs and semipalmated plover. Their nests are often little more than depressions in the ground. During nesting season greater yellowlegs frequent wet bogs, often finding a vantage point from which to hurl themselves at an intruder while uttering shrill notes of alarm. Plovers feign injury to draw an intruder from eggs or newly hatched young.

Estuaries, lakes, ponds, and large rivers are the primary habitat of the all-white trumpeter swan, largest North American waterfowl and the rarest swan. In 1980, 20 trumpeters were counted in the Chilkat Valley.

One pair has successfully reared young in a nest on the west bank of

Trumpeter swans, largest of North America's waterfowl, nest along the Chilkat River, southernmost of known nesting areas for this species. Head and neck feathers of swans sometimes become stained from iron in the water while the birds are feeding. (Helen Rhode)

(Above) Largest of the continent's passerines, the resourceful and adaptable raven makes its home in the Chilkat Valley. Southeast also shelters the raven's smaller relative, the crow. (Doug Murphy)

(Below) Woodland birds of the area include the American robin, one of seven thrushes found in Alaska. (Helen Rhode)

the Chilkat River for more than a decade. It was not until 1979 that a second known pair reared a brood near the Chilkat River. Three breeding pairs were present in 1980. This is the southernmost known nesting area for trumpeter swans in Alaska. Biologists do not know why the local population has not increased more rapidly.

Any swans seen in the Chilkat Valley are probably trumpeters. Tundra swans (formerly called whistling swans) migrate through the area in October. They look much like trumpeters but are smaller and have a higher-pitched call.

One of the more remarkable permanent residents is the plump, slate-colored northern dipper or water ouzel. Most common in mountain streams, the northern dipper will be found in almost all parts of Alaska where there is open, running water. Although they are songbirds with a clear, silvery voice, dippers walk along the bottoms of streams probing for aquatic insects or larvae. They build their nests near streams or beneath waterfalls where the nests will be camouflaged and constantly wet.

Tiniest of the forest inhabitants is the rufous hummingbird, which migrates to its Southeast breeding ground in April and early May. The vibrating sound of its wings is sometimes the first clue to its presence.

The omnipresent common raven, largest North American passerine, figures prominently in Tlingit legends and art.

Other woodland birds found in the Chilkat Valley include chestnut-backed chickadee, American robin, varied thrush, hermit thrush, ruby-crowned kinglet, Bohemian waxwing, common redpoll, pine siskin, dark-eyed (Oregon) junco, Lincoln's sparrow, and song sparrow. Four warblers nest in the woodlands: orange-crowned, yellow-rumped, Townsend's, and Wilson's.

Blue grouse inhabit the dense spruce-hemlock forest throughout the year. Brush forms such an abundant cover that these upland birds are rarely seen. In spring they are most readily identified by the muffled hooting notes made by the male during courtship.

When startled, blue grouse take off with a roar of wings. In late summer and fall they often feed on berries and insects at timberline. With cold weather they move into the woods and live to a considerable extent on buds and needles of conifers.

Ninety-four bald eagle nests have been counted in the Chilkat Valley, probably the highest known inland

nesting density for this compelling bird.

But even more significant for the eagles is a gathering so spectacular that its meeting place has been named the Council Grounds. Between October and February of each year some 3,500 eagles assemble along a three- to five-mile stretch of the Chilkat River, creating the world's largest known concentration of bald eagles. The Haines Highway runs adjacent to their gathering place on the river near Klukwan, making it one of the most accessible wildlife dramas anywhere.

The great birds line trees and river bars in numbers that satiate the senses, taking scant notice of bird-watchers in their midst. They soar on thermals hundreds at a time, climbing to mere specks in binoculars.

Eagles descend from their roosts in cottonwood trees along the banks of the Chilkat River near Klukwan to feed on frozen spawned-out chum salmon.
(George Figdor)

What attracts eagles in unheard-of numbers are the major fall runs of chum salmon. At the confluence of the Chilkat and Tsirku rivers warm groundwater discharges upward into

the Chilkat River at about 40° F, protecting sections of the river from freezeup. Open water supports the later salmon run, which in turn provides plentiful meals for eagles during an otherwise lean time of year. Shallow, braided river channels make decaying fish easy prey, and black cottonwood trees along the bank offer a ready site for perching and roosting.

The Council Grounds are believed to attract eagles from throughout Southeast and British Columbia. Summer finds the birds dispersed through this area. In fall, when a low-pressure area and southerly winds bring warmer weather, the eagles move north toward the Chilkat.

Northerly winds and colder temperatures drive other eagles south toward the same area. They start assembling in October, at first scattered throughout the Chilkat watershed, but especially along the Klehini River. Then they concentrate on the Council Grounds.

After January brings winter with a vengeance, radio-tracked birds are traced as far as the Washington-Oregon border, 1,200 miles south of Haines.

Mature bald eagles share a perch in an old cottonwood at the Council Grounds along the Chilkat River. (Third Eye Photography)

48

The mature bald eagle is as unmistakable as it is impressive. The showy snow white head and tail clearly assert the identity of the majestic bird which has been alternately admired and vilified for centuries. In the juvenile dress of its first four years, the bald eagle is an all-over mottled brown and easily confused with the North American golden eagle.

There are perhaps 30,000 bald eagles in Alaska, more than in all other states combined. About half of these live in Southeast, where more than 4,000 nests have been recorded along the shorelines.

Eagles nest in old-growth trees along the coast and larger mainland rivers, in trees both tall enough to grant unobstructed view of the fish that feed them and sturdy enough to support their massive nests. When spawning salmon are not available, eagles use their curved talons and hooked beaks for catching and tearing herring, cod, flounder, clams, crabs, and a variety of waterfowl, birds, and small mammals.

Nests are used for many years, growing by additional limbs and twigs with each use until they reach as much as three to five feet deep and four to seven feet in diameter. Nest

live salmon, their main food supply is spawned-out salmon.

Bald eagles and their nest trees have been protected in Alaska since 1959 under federal law. Alaska, and especially the Chilkat Valley, remain the last stronghold of the national emblem.

Some now envision the Chilkat Valley as a major center for bald eagle research and education. There could be an observatory along the Chilkat River where bird-watchers and photographers could pursue their activities sheltered from chilling winds, rain, and snow, and without unduly disturbing the birds. Local eagles could be used to restore former ranges throughout the United States.

"It could rival Mount McKinley as an attraction and educational tool," says 20-year Haines resident David Olerud.

The concept is a new one for a community once bitterly torn by the abundance of the national emblem in its midst. In the late 1970s potential logging and mining activity drew attention from conservationists concerned about threats to fisheries and eagle habitat. For a city historically beset by economic downturns — a succession of closures by fish canneries, gold mine operations, the army base, a private orphanage — the eagle seemed to

building begins in March. Two or three white eggs are laid in a shallow depression, hatching by late May or early June. Eaglets are fully feathered and ready for flight by mid-August.

Once found throughout North America, the bald eagle has fallen victim to hunting, poaching, chemical destruction, and human encroachment of habitat. A bounty system took a heavy toll of eagles between 1917 and 1952. Fishermen once believed that eagles competed with them for salmon. Although eagles will feed on

50

threaten the timber industry and deal the town yet another blow.

In 1979 the National Audubon Society initiated a four-year study in conjunction with the U.S. Fish and Wildlife Service to learn how the eagle could be protected while other resources were developed. The Audubon Society sent Erv Boeker, a retired Fish and Wildlife biologist, to Haines to head the research.

On June 15, 1982, former governor Jay Hammond traveled to Haines to sign into law a bill establishing the 49,000-acre Alaska Chilkat Bald Eagle Preserve. Traditional public uses such as hunting, fishing, trapping, harvest of personal firewood, use of motorized vehicles, and other recreation and subsistence activities will be allowed in the preserve. Access to private lands and valid mining claims or mineral leases is assured. The preserve is closed, however, to mineral entry, commercial timber harvest, and sale of land under the state land disposal program.

The bill also created Alaska's first state forest, the Haines State Forest Resource Management Area, where commercial harvest of timber is allowed.

A 12-member advisory council was named with representatives from the city and borough of Haines, state and federal resource agencies, and from

local Native, fishing, conservation, and development interests. The preserve is included in the Alaska state park system, and the council will assist the Division of Parks in developing within two years a management plan for the preserve. Special attention will be given the 5,000 acres within the preserve on which eagles depend during coldest winter periods.

The Chilkat experience has been hailed as a model for resolving conflicts over multiple resource use in other areas.

One Haines resident with high hopes for what the eagle can mean to the town's economic future is David Olerud, a sporting goods merchant.

Haines resident David Olerud proudly displays his limited edition rifle made by U.S. Repeating Arms Company during the bicentennial year of the bald eagle as the national bird. (Jim Rearden)

For the 200th anniversary of the eagle as national emblem in 1982, he persuaded U.S. Repeating Arms to issue a commemorative bald eagle Winchester rifle. In the process he also helped found the American Bald Eagle Foundation. With proceeds from sale of the rifle and other commemorative items and with private contributions, the foundation seeks to finance a research and visitor center.

Agriculture

Most Chilkat Valley households cultivate kitchen gardens for personal use. Some still produce the mammoth sweet strawberries developed by Charlie Anway in the early 1900s.

Gone are the dairy farms of earlier decades, but Harriett Jurgeleit, executive director of the Southeast Alaska State Fair, notes a renewed interest in agriculture among valley residents. The fair is an annual showcase for flowers, vegetables, preserved foods, and other home arts produced around Southeast. Farm animals are brought in for the exhibition the third weekend of each August. The 21-acre fairground about a mile from downtown Haines had nearly 12,000 visitors in 1982. In 1983 the Southeast Alaska State Fair marked its 15th anniversary. The fair annually draws both exhibitors and spectators from Whitehorse, Yukon Territory, as well as the Chilkat Valley, Skagway, Gustavus, Sitka, Juneau, and as far away as Ketchikan.

Mrs. Jurgeleit came to Haines as a 15-year-old to visit her aunt, Harriett Lawrence, administrator at Haines House. She simply stayed on, living with her aunt at the foster home. When Haines House was in full operation between 1921 and 1960,

A garden near Klukwan supports a flourishing crop of carrots, lettuce, broccoli, and other vegetables. (Dave Mills)

Two young gardeners inspect a patch of impressive cabbages which are ready to be harvested. (George Figdor)

(Above) *Crowds throng to the Southeast Alaska State Fair held each year in August. The fair celebrated its 15th anniversary in 1983.* (John Svenson)

(Right) *A visitor to the Southeast Alaska State Fair at Haines purchases locally grown carrots at the fair's farmer's market.* (George Figdor)

Misty, half Percheron and half bronco, gives David Woodring (right) and Robert Ranck a ride aboard a scoot. David, who passed away in December 1982, and his wife, Janet, farmed five and one-half acres along the Haines Highway for many years. Misty, who died in 1983, was one of the few draft horses in Southeast. (Janet Woodring)

staff and residents grew vegetables for their own use and operated a dairy farm with barn and silo. Farmland tilled by the institution is now built up within the city, she says.

Charlie Anway crossed strains of strawberries to produce the winner that bears his name. Specimens preserved in formaldehyde won honorable mention in the 1909 Alaska-Yukon-Pacific Exposition in Seattle. What he developed was a berry that could grow big as a lemon, yet remain red to the center, firm and sweet.

After Anway's death in 1949, Mary Meacock started caring for his plants to preserve them. For the next two decades she shipped berries and plants throughout Southeast and the Lower 48. The Anway strawberries will attain their famous size in other parts of Alaska, she says, but not in other states.

"It's daylight all night," she says of their success in Alaska. "Nothing knows when to quit growing."

Mrs. Meacock cared for as much as one acre of strawberries, cultivating plants and cutting runners in spring. Requests for the plants still come in, but now would-be growers are invited to dig their own.

Anway also started cherry and apple trees on his land at Piedad Road north of town. Bing, Royal Ann, Lambert, Black Republican, and Pie cherries all did well under the husbandry of Mrs. Meacock for 25 years, until a fickle warm spell in March caused sap to rise and the ensuing freeze split trees wide open. Apples — Northern Spy, Waxen, Winter Banana, Yellow Transparent, Siberian Crab — thrive on what was once the Anway farm, as do gooseberries, raspberries, and currants.

Once again a religious community in the valley is attempting to produce food for its own use. Mount Bether Bible Center at Mile 26.5 Haines Highway is using a greenhouse to augment its vegetable garden. Extra potatoes are sold or used in their downtown restaurant. A few years ago a barn fire wiped out the community's cows, chickens, and goats, reducing current livestock to a few pigs. Members plan to replenish the animals as they are able.

Fish/Fishing

The entire Chilkat Valley is fish habitat, with virtually every stream and river either a salmon spawning stream or tributary to a spawning stream.

All five species of eastern Pacific salmon are found here: king, coho, sockeye, pink, and chum. Numerous other species — Dolly Varden; cutthroat, steelhead, and brook trout; arctic grayling; whitefish; eulachon — share the region's waterways.

The Lynn Canal fishery is one of the largest and most stable fisheries in Southeast, providing employment for commercial fishermen throughout the region as well as local residents. Sea and inland waters provide fish for subsistence and personal use and for sport anglers. Nearly everyone in the Chilkat Valley fishes at least for personal use.

January through May, while waters of the Chilkat River run clear and free from glacial silt, Dolly Varden are available for sportfishing in the

A fisherman dips for eulachon, a bluish silver smeltlike fish, in the Chilkat River. In years past, Tlingits rendered oil from these fish to preserve food, to eat as a dip, and to trade. (John Svenson)

55

Chilkat River. Winter months also offer good ice fishing for Dolly Varden and cutthroat trout on Mosquito Lake and Chilkat Lake.

Mid-May brings a short run of eulachon up the Chilkat and Chilkoot rivers. The bluish silver smeltlike fish have been important to Tlingit Indians for centuries, and they continue to be harvested for subsistence use.

A king salmon run follows the eulachon, continuing until mid-June. Each year the Haines Sportsmen's Association sponsors a five-day salmon derby during the Memorial Day holiday weekend and the following weekend. Entrants come from as far as Juneau to angle for the largest kings, which traditionally weigh 35 to 55 pounds.

From mid-June through early August, sockeye salmon run up the Chilkoot side of the valley, followed by pinks. September brings the fall run, which peaks about October 1. Cohos run on the Chilkoot side about four weeks. In the Chilkat drainage where stretches of water never freeze,

Calm waters of Chilkat Inlet belie the surging life underneath the surface where all five species of eastern Pacific salmon and numerous other species of fish either head for the fresh water of the Chilkat Valley or spend their life in the depths of Lynn Canal. (Matthew Donohoe)

(Above) Boats line up Memorial Day weekend for the opening of the five-day salmon derby at Haines. (Shelley Stallings)

(Left) Terry Friske and his son share a proud moment by displaying their king salmon catch. (Shelley Stallings)

57

Judson Cranston, Sr., and his wife display fish strips cut from salmon caught in the Chilkat. The Chilkat Valley is prime fish habitat where most streams serve either as spawning grounds or tributaries to spawning grounds. (Larry McNeil Photography, courtesy of Sealaska Corporation)

cohos and chum continue to run through the end of the year.

A ban on foreign fishing within 200 miles of the United States coastline, and short commercial seasons for Alaska fishermen, have allowed deep-water halibut to migrate far into Lynn Canal in recent years. This has increased opportunities for halibut sportfishing near Haines from mid-July through September.

The Chilkat River continues to yield salmon and eulachon for subsistence use, as it has for countless years. Subsistence set gill nets take salmon from the Chilkat in the only subsistence set-net fishery in Southeast. The state has issued about 320 subsistence permits for the Chilkat River.

Set nets rest perpendicularly in the river water, with floats along the upper edge and lead line or sinkers along the bottom. One end of the net is staked to the shore, the other floats in an eddy where fish like to gather. Salmon swimming into the net are caught by the gills.

Drift nets may be used for subsistence fishing in salt water when commercial fishing seasons are open.

Eulachon are scooped from the Chilkoot and Chilkat rivers with dip nets during their brief run. Many years ago Tlingits rendered fish oil by placing eulachon in a pit dug near the river, then leaving the fish to ripen for 10 to 14 days. Hot water and hot rocks were added to the pit and oil was skimmed from the top as it rose. By the late 1880s, pits were replaced by canoes half-buried in the sand. A medium-sized canoe filled with fish would yield five to six gallons of oil. When cauldrons became available, the yield of oil was greatly increased by adding ripened fish to boiling water.

Before other preserving methods

Archie Klaney, who relies on fish as a major portion of his diet, rows against a turbulent current on the Chilkat near Klukwan. (Larry McNeil Photography, courtesy of Sealaska Corporation)

A man and woman dip net for hooligan (eulachon) along the Chilkat River, north of Haines. The fruit of their labor, shown below, is prized by the Tlingit people, who harvest the tiny fish each spring and render them for their oil. (Both by George Figdor)

Lillian Hammond cooks hooligan in a large vat at a fish camp (below), skimming off the valuable oil after several hours of cooking (bottom).
(Both by George Figdor)

were available, oil was poured over berries in containers to seal out air. Oil was used for frying, eaten as a dip much like drawn butter, added to berries for flavor, drunk at feasts. The dried fish are so oily they can be burned for light, earning them the nickname candlefish.

Haines's resident fleet of about 60 commercial gill-netters can often harvest their salmon catch just a few miles from home. In season the hometown fleet swells with fishermen from the West Coast and other parts of Southeast.

The Lynn Canal commercial fishery is generally increasing, because of good winter survival rates in recent years and good escapement levels. The 1982 sockeye harvest set an

all-time record with 280,000 fish. Chum salmon harvest peaked in 1974 at 450,000 fish, then fell into a slump in the late 1970s. It has started to rebuild, and in 1982 the chum harvest reached 300,000 fish. Pink salmon have become more important in recent years, with harvests of 75,000 in 1982 and 120,000 in 1981.

Commercial fishing boats and pleasure craft tie up at the small-boat harbor at Haines. The Lynn Canal fishery in nearby waters is one of the largest and most stable in Southeast. (K.R. Kollodge)

In earlier years, 20,000 to 30,000 pinks would have been a typical harvest. The coho harvest has remained fairly stable, and the 1982 harvest of 70,000 was third highest in 10 years.

Most of the gill-net fleet heads for Icy Strait and Cross Sound to fish for halibut in spring. Some trollers are based in Haines, but recent restrictions have diminished participation in this fishery.

Shrimp and crab inhabit local waters, but not in the concentrations found off western Alaska. Severe weather during winter months and remoteness from buyers limit the shellfish fleet to the most determined.

During a lifetime of commercial fishing, 54-year-old Charles Clayton has seen a succession of changes. Nylon nets have replaced linen nets, power-operated gill nets have mechanized the back-breaking work of hauling in nets by hand. Restrictions on length and location of fisheries have complicated the fisherman's lot, but are helping assure better escapements, he says.

Clayton's first boat and net cost $800; his new 36-foot aluminum FV *Exemption* cost $80,000. The limited entry gill-net permit he holds now has a market value of $40,000 to $45,000. Clayton also has a nontransferable trolling permit.

Perhaps the first commercial fish processing began centuries ago when Chilkat and Chilkoot Indians used the rendered eulachon oil for trade with interior Indians. The first canneries, however, date back just a century. Two canneries opened on the shores of Chilkat Inlet, one in 1882 and one in 1883. By 1900, Chilkoot Inlet also supported two canneries. In early years thousands of Chinese laborers were imported from the West Coast to work in canneries.

Campers at Rainbow Glacier Camp can still swim among pilings which supported the Alaska Fishermen's Union cannery at Madsen's Cove around the turn of the century. The building was torn down around 1908, and materials were transported to Excursion Inlet at the southeast corner of Glacier Bay for a cannery there.

In 1917 Tim Vogel constructed a cannery in Letnikof Cove, south of Haines on the west side of the Chilkat Peninsula. It was sold and renamed Haines Packing Company in 1936, and remains the oldest continuing business in the Haines area. The company now buys fish for processing at Excursion Inlet.

Haines fisherman Dean Walsh pitches a sockeye salmon from his boat, the Red Witch. (Shelley Stallings)

Fishermen arrange nets at the Haines boat harbor. Revenue from fishing offsets some of the ups and downs of the area's economy. (Janet Woodring)

There is no cannery in operation in the Chilkat Valley today. Tenders buy fish and haul them to canneries elsewhere. Nevertheless, local fish processing is undergoing something of a rebirth.

Don and Betty Holgate and their family moved to Haines in 1973 from Rhode Island, where they had owned and operated a shipyard for 16 years. In 1982 they began freezing fish in a walk-in plant behind their Mud Bay Road home. They also smoke salmon and hold an on-board processing license for the *Cap'n. J.E. Clark.*

In the year-round family operation they freeze halibut, all species of salmon, king and tanner crab, and shrimp. Even during their first year, word-of-mouth endorsements brought orders from as far as the East Coast.

"People would stop by, buy a small chunk and charcoal it on the beach, then come back for more. That's what I want to develop," says Betty Holgate. "I want a reputation for a quality product."

Halibut is frozen whole to a temperature of minus 30° F, then cut with a meat saw and packed in

Haines Packing Company, oldest continuing business in the Haines area, still operates a facility on Letnikof Cove where the company buys fish for processing at Excursion Inlet.
(J. Schultz)

polypropylene. Whole salmon is glazed in ice water without chemicals. An automated smoker processes sockeye and chum salmon.

Betty Holgate is also writing a seafood recipe pamphlet to combat the tendency to overcook and overseason seafood. She has found that people more accustomed to breaded fish sticks from the grocery store barely know what to do when

The Holgate family operates the Cap'n J.E. Clark, *a gill-netter which fishes Lynn Canal. Don and Betty Holgate also run a plant near their Mud Bay Road home for freezing halibut, salmon, crab, and shrimp.*
(Shelley Stallings)

Gill-netters, part of the Haines fleet, are hauled up on shore for winter storage at Letnikof Cove. (Matthew Donohoe)

confronted with a whole halibut, king crab, or shrimp, or how to recognize a quality product.

"Someone even thought halibut was supposed to be yellow."

Clams and mussels are found on local beaches, but because of the risk of paralytic shellfish poisoning (PSP), no Southeast beaches are at this time approved for shellfish harvest for human consumption.

The toxin from PSP causes tingling and numbness in lips, gums, tongue, and face followed by similar sensations in fingers and toes. In severe cases, complete muscular paralysis in the extremities and neck result in respiratory failure. If symptoms appear, vomiting should be induced immediately and a rapid laxative should be used, followed by medical care as soon as possible.

The poison, invisible, tasteless, and odorless, is not destroyed by cooking. There is no known antidote.

Transportation Corridor

For unknown centuries the Chilkat Valley has been a chink in the wall of mountains, a gateway between the sea and landlocked interior regions. It provided a valued and fiercely guarded route for transportation and commerce.

Ganaxtedih and Daklawedih Ravens, local Indian tribes, owned trading trails to middle Yukon fur country over Chilkat Pass; and from the head of the Chilkat River, over a glacier, to the Takhini River, and on to the Yukon. The Indians controlled the routes through their fortified village at Klukwan. Ravens of Chilkoot and Yendestakyeh owned trails over Chilkoot and White passes to lakes forming the headwaters of the Yukon River.

Control of these routes through otherwise impassable mountain ranges gave warriors and traders a monopoly on trade with Gunanas or "Stick Indians" in the middle and upper

Intrepid travelers ford a river along the Dalton Trail. Dalton charged a toll for people and animals using the trail: $1.00 per foot passenger, $10.00 for a four-horse team and wagon. Sheep, goats, and swine cost $.25 a head. (Yukon Archives, MacBride Museum Collection, Vol. I)

Yukon Basin. These Indians first acquired the products of western civilization via the waters of Lynn Canal.

The arrival of white men cast the Chilkats in the role of middlemen, and they devised elaborate trading parties of up to 100 men and lasting a

month or more. Products sought by the Gunanas included tobacco, sugar, flour, woolen blankets, gunpowder, lead, and colored fabrics. Chilkats obtained these products from white traders. Chilkats also traded eulachon oil they rendered, giving the trails the nickname of grease trails.

From the interior they brought back moose hides, furs, dried meats, jade tools, copper, decorated moccasins, birch bows wound with porcupine gut, and prepared caribou hides.

In 1852, Chilkats learned Fort Selkirk had been erected at the junction of the Yukon and Pelly rivers in Yukon Territory to control fur trade in that area. Koh-Klux', a famous Chilkat chief, and his people promptly destroyed the fort and gave notice another should not be built.

The wedge that finally cracked the impenetrable gate was gold. The Dyea-Chilkoot route was first opened to a party of 20 American prospectors in 1880, with the understanding the prospectors would not in any way meddle with Indian fur trade. Every year thereafter, miners challenged the dangers of the Dyea Trail and

Lowlands of the Chilkat River provide access to the mountain barrier surrounding Lynn Canal. Prospectors found a way through the mountains in their quest to reach gold strikes in the Interior. (George Wuerthner)

Chilkoot Pass. The Klondike stampede began less than 20 years later, and trade came under control of United States and Canadian customs officials. The ancient trade monopoly had been destroyed.

A toll road of sorts between Pyramid Harbor and Fort Selkirk was developed by Jack Dalton, who came

Jack Dalton arrived in Haines in the late 1800s from where he began work on the Dalton Trail, a 300-mile route from Pyramid Harbor on Lynn Canal through the mountains to Fort Selkirk, on the Yukon River, not far upstream from the discoveries of the Klondike. (Yukon Archives, MacBride Museum Collection, Vol. I)

to Haines in the 1880s or early 1890s with a questionable but colorful background. He had reportedly been a Cherokee Strip, Oklahoma, cowboy who worked his way up to Oregon, then left to avoid prosecution for shooting scrapes. During the time he was laying out the 300-mile Dalton Trail in 1893, he was accused and acquitted of the murder of Daniel McGinnis at Chilkat.

Dalton's route to the Yukon was longer than Chilkoot and White Pass trails, but not as physically

demanding. Way stations were established every 20 miles, and bridges were in place for operation by 1896. A toll was charged for passage of people and animals, although Dalton did not acquire federal sanction for a toll road until March 1899. Natives were exempt from fee.

One foot passenger with a pack was charged $1.00. An unloaded sled or wagon with a single horse cost $2.50; a four-horse team with one wagon cost $10.00. Additional cattle, horses, and mules were assessed $2.50 each,

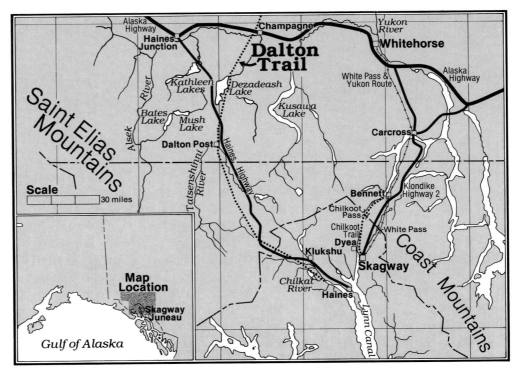

while sheep, goats, and swine could pass for $.25 a head. The Dalton Trail Company, which included J.F. Mahoney and F.D. Nowell of Juneau, operated its toll route from mid-June through mid-September.

Overnight stopping places included Chilkat Lake and the town of Porcupine, where Dalton started a trading company and acquired gold claims in 1899.

Most of Dalton's roadhouses along the route were tents. Known roadhouses were located at Walkerville, Dalton Cache, Three Guardsmen Pass, Glacier Camp and Bear Camp, Dalton Post, and Mush Lake. Other roadhouses probably existed beyond this point, as the trail extended 175 miles farther into Yukon Territory.

Sometime around or before 1896, Dalton also constructed a trading post at Mile 42 on the Haines Highway, at Pleasant Camp, where the United States and Canadian borders now meet.

Dalton Cache has been remodeled

Most of the rest stops Jack Dalton built along his 300-mile trail were tent camps like this one at Walkerville. (H.C. Barley Collection, #4696, Yukon Archives)

extensively through the years. Recently it was placed on the National Register of Historic Places. Its location between American and Canadian customs stations makes it an ideal site for a visitor and interpretative center, according to BLM officials who would like to pass Dalton Cache to the state for refurbishing and operation. The state of Alaska has not funded the project, however, and the building remains boarded up in the custody of the federal government.

Traces of the Dalton Trail can still be found on both sides of the Klehini River, indicating the trail shifted depending on high and low water conditions. When the current Haines Highway was extended to Pleasant Camp in 1926, the last three miles followed a section of the Dalton Trail. Dalton built his trail for packhorses and ox carts, and some turns too sharp for cars were eventually removed. Beyond Pleasant Camp in Canada, the Haines Highway roughly parallels and occasionally crosses the Dalton Trail.

In 1897 there was also high interest in a rail line from Portage Cove to the site of Fort Selkirk, but the scheme by Humbert Railway Expedition collapsed the following spring. Ten years later the Alaska Midland Railway to Fairbanks was proposed. But when the Alaska Railroad Bill was passed, Seward, not Haines, was chosen as tidewater terminus.

Advent of World War II and location of Fort William H. Seward, established around the turn of the century, on coastal waters gave new impetus to an overland link. A road that would connect Alaska to the Lower 48 had

been under governmental consideration since 1930, but no action was taken until both Canada and the United States saw the road as a defense measure 10 years later. The bombing of Pearl Harbor and threatened closure of sea lanes to Alaska added urgency, and in February 1942 officials decided the highway should follow a chain of airfields across western Canada and Alaska. In 1943 the road north of Haines was extended to meet the newly constructed Alaska Highway, making it possible to drive from Haines to Miami, Florida.

Dalton Cache, one of the posts built by Jack Dalton to serve travelers along the Dalton Trail, has recently undergone restoration under supervision of the Bureau of Land Management. The cache is listed on the National Register of Historic Places.
(John Beck, BLM)

The Haines Highway passes through a sparsely populated portion of British Columbia, but it has forged strong bonds between the people of the Chilkat Valley and nearby Yukon Territory. Haines residents readily make the 257-mile drive to Whitehorse for shopping and services

in all seasons. Ron and Phyllis Martin of Haines venture that when they owned a motel, 75 percent of their guests came from Canada. A 363-mile northern loop through Canada takes motorists from Haines back to Alaska to link with the roadways of Interior and Southcentral.

To the south, Haines is joined with the remainder of Southeast via the Alaska Marine Highway. The ferry system was an early dream of Steve Homer. He purchased a landing craft, named it the *Chilkoot,* and in 1948 began passenger service between Skagway, Haines, and Juneau. His first passengers were Territorial Governor Ernest Gruening and Judge Simon Hellenthal. Homer sold his ferry to the territory of Alaska after four years, running it for them another year. It proved practical enough that a special small ship, the *Chilkat,* was built in 1957.

By the time Alaska became a state in 1959 the concept of a marine highway had been proven in Southeast. Haines now has a new ferry terminal and is one of more than a dozen Southeast communities with regularly scheduled service. Car-carrying ferries make it possible to drive between Southeast and other portions of the state or the Lower 48 by combining road miles with a scenic cruise.

Completion of a road from Skagway to Carcross in 1979 opened a circle trip with 13-mile ferry link between Haines and Skagway via Warm Pass, Carcross, Whitehorse, Champagne, Canyon, Haines Junction, and Dezadeash, all in Canada, before returning to Alaska at Pleasant Camp.

For some years, primarily in an effort to make the capital city of Juneau more accessible to the remainder of the state, there has been talk of shortening the ferry link between Haines and Juneau by extending the Haines Highway south to Saint James Bay.

The proposed 55-mile extension would follow the west shore of Lynn Canal at the base of the Chilkat Range. Shuttle ferries would transfer traffic across Lynn Canal to a terminal

at Echo Cove north of Juneau. Potential routes were first studied in 1963. A road down the east side of Lynn Canal was dismissed as impractical because of its steep, rocky terrain, wide low river valleys, and glaciers.

Another proposal to link Juneau with the state's highway system at Haines would require a short ferry run across Lynn Canal from Berners Bay, north of Juneau, to William Henry Bay. From there a road would run north past Davidson Glacier to a point near Haines, thus providing access to the Haines Highway.

Similar proposals seek to connect Haines and Skagway by road, but extremely rugged terrain creates engineering and financial obstacles which have prevented construction of such a route.

Haines is also accessible by air. Air carriers offer daily scheduled flights between Haines and Juneau.

Modes of transportation and merchandise have changed, but the role of the Chilkat Valley has not. It remains a corridor for the passage of people and goods in daily commerce.

The Haines Highway follows the Chilkat River for part of its 151-mile run from Haines to join the Alaska Highway at Haines Junction, Yukon Territory. (Matthew Donohoe)

Boundary Dispute

Fixing the boundaries of what would become southeastern Alaska involved off-and-on political maneuvering spanning three-quarters of a century.

First to wrestle with the complexities of dividing an area unsurveyed, unmapped, and little used were the English and the Russians, in the Treaty of 1825. Negotiations between Britain and Russia placed the boundary on the crest of mountains nearest the sea, or along the coast no farther than 10 leagues (30 nautical miles) from the ocean.

Russians were piqued at the 10-league limitation. In 1826 they published a map showing the entire boundary about 10 leagues from the coast, even though some mountain crests would place it closer to the sea. There was no British protest to the map, and the map line was the boundary for the territory the United States understood it had purchased from Russia in 1867. William Seward, secretary of state, ordered publication of a map closely following the Russian map line, and for the next two decades it was copied by cartographers around the world. Seward had visited the Chilkat Valley in 1869, the same year George Davidson traveled up the Chilkat River to Klukwan to observe a solar eclipse.

So long as the boundary area was used primarily by Indians and fur traders, precise location mattered little. As economic, social, and religious development grew, so did the need for a fixed boundary.

Within five years after the United States purchased Russian America, pressure for a boundary settlement came from British Columbia because of a gold strike in the north Cassiar district.

President U.S. Grant recommended to Congress in 1872 the appointment

Visitors traveling the Haines Highway must stop at the Canada customs and immigration offices at Pleasant Camp, about 40 miles from Haines. (J. Schultz)

1. Lord Alverstone.	6. George Turner.	11. David T. Watson.	16. Robert Lansing.	21. H. C. McArthur.	26. R. C. Proctor.
2. Elihu Root.	7. John W Foster.	12. Christopher Robinson.	17. L. P. Duff.	22. Otis T. Cartwright.	27. C F. Robertson.
3. H. C. Lodge.	8. Clifford Sifton.	13. Hannis Taylor.	18. S. A. T. Rowlatt.	23. T. John Newton.	28. Reginald Tower.
4. Sir Louis Jette.	9. J. M. Dickinson.	14. F. C. Wade.	19. A. Geoffrion.	24. F. R. Hanna.	29. J. Ridgely Carter.
5. Allen B. Aylesworth.	10. Sir Robert Finlay.	15. Chandler P. Anderson.	20. W. C. Hodgkins.	25. L. P. Marvin.	30. J. Pope.

AMERICA WINS THE ALASKA BOUNDARY AWARD

The claim of the United States to the disputed Alaska territory was confirmed, with the exception of one concession to Canada, by the Commission sitting in London. The photograph shows the final session of the Tribunal at the Foreign Office

of a commission to determine the boundary while sparse population lessened the likelihood of border conflict. Congress did not act on the costly proposal. Then Britain proposed marking points on rivers, but even this was rejected as too expensive.

Decline of the Cassiar fields temporarily lessened pressure for the boundary settlement.

In 1885 Pres. Grover Cleveland recommended a preliminary survey; again Congress did nothing.

One Canadian study commission argued not only that the correct location was on mountaintops nearest the sea, but that the "coast" should refer to the ocean, not to the coast of inlets. Thus the boundary line would cross through inlets, not go around their heads.

When news of spectacular gold discoveries in the Klondike reached Seattle in July 1897, thousands of miners from around the world headed north and the boundary again became an issue.

A Joint High Commission met in 1898-99 to settle the question. Canada advanced the claim by British Columbia that would give Canada the heads of inlets; the United States argued that its border would be merely disconnected promontories.

After the 1898 presidential election, serious negotiations began. The United States consented to a Canadian proposal for a port at Pyramid Harbor. It would be under nominal sovereignty of the United States so long as Canada maintained customs and police posts at the harbor. Canada suggested that the general boundary fall midway between the boundaries claimed by Canada and the United States.

The proposal leaked out and caused such a storm of protest in the western states that the American delegation withdrew the Pyramid Harbor offer, and the High Commission broke down in 1899.

Secretary of State John Hay tried to arrange a temporary boundary on Chilkat Pass, particularly at Porcupine Creek where many American miners had come to escape a British Columbia law requiring miners to be naturalized. In 1899 a provisional boundary was drawn along the south side of the Klehini River, placing Porcupine within the United States.

Resolution was finally on the way in 1903 with the signing of a boundary convention. A tribunal of six jurists was to decide on a boundary based on arguments and evidence, considering the treaties of 1825 and 1867 and the actions of governments showing their interpretation of the location of boundaries.

Appointed to represent the United States were Senator Henry Cabot Lodge, Senator George Turner of Washington State, and Secretary of War Elihu Root. Representing Britain were Lord Alverston, Lord Chief Justice of England and president of the Alaska Boundary Tribunal; Sir Louis Jette, lieutenant governor of Quebec and a former member of the Supreme Court; and Justice George Armour, member of the Supreme Court of Canada. After Armour's death, he was replaced by a Toronto lawyer, Allen B. Aylesworth.

The tribunal convened at 11:00 A.M. September 3, 1903, in the Foreign Office, London. Much of its attention focused on the division of islands at the entrance of Portland Canal which forms the southeastern boundary of Southeast. It was finally agreed smaller Sitklan and Kanagunut islands would go to the United States while Pearse and Wales islands went to Canada. In the Chilkat Valley a line was drawn between Pleasant Camp, manned by the North West Mounted Police, and Dalton Cache.

When the agreement was signed on October 20, 1903, the boundary in the valley extended 20 miles beyond the temporary boundary at the Klehini River. It was nearly a reassertion of the line drawn on a map by Russians 77 years earlier.

Church

Haines traces both its name and its townsite to missionary activities of the Presbyterian Church.

Chilkat village chiefs met in 1879 with delegates from the church to discuss a site where a mission might be established. Representing the church were the Reverend S. Hall Young and his naturalist friend, John Muir. On this trip Muir first explored Glacier Bay before going with Young to Chilkat country.

The location they chose for the mission was called Dei Shu, meaning "end of the trail." The area was often used to portage canoes between the Chilkat River and Chilkoot Inlet but had no permanent settlement. Later the name was changed to Haines, honoring Mrs. F.E.H. Haines, a member of the Presbyterian Board of Home Missions.

The Reverend Eugene S. Willard and his wife, Caroline, came as the first missionaries in 1881 and began developing a boarding school and a small church. When they moved from Haines in 1885, operation of the school was transferred to the federal government. Mrs. Willard describes her days in the Chilkat Valley in her book *Life in Alaska* (1884). In 1907, when the government built its own school, the original school building became a hospital and functioned until 1918.

One of the teachers attracted by the school was Solomon Ripinski, a widely traveled Polish Jew who spent the rest of his life in Haines. Arriving in 1886, he was the first permanent trader in Haines as well as teacher, surveyor, jurist, bookkeeper, postmaster, and mapmaker. Mount Ripinski (3,600 feet) just north of Haines bears his name.

Between 1921 and 1960 the

In 1879 the Reverend S. Hall Young and John Muir met with the Chilkat chiefs to choose a site for building a Presbyterian mission in the Chilkat Valley. This sketch by an unknown artist of the original buildings at Haines Mission appeared in Frank Leslie's Illustrated Newspaper, *May 20, 1882.*
(Reprinted from *ALASKA SPORTSMAN*)

Presbyterian mission operated Haines House, a foster home for children. The former hospital building was remodeled and soon overflowed with children. By 1927 a second three-story building was constructed, doubling the capacity of Haines House. Through the years a farm with dairy herd and extensive gardens were added to provide food for the home.

In the mid-1950s the home began to shift toward a pre-delinquent remedial center, but neither staff nor community was able to meet the demands of staffing, maintenance, and insurance that followed. The Board of National Missions elected to close Haines House. The buildings were razed, and a new church was built on the site.

Today the Presbyterian Board of National Missions retains 49 acres of the 366 acres to which it received occupancy rights in 1896. Other parcels were sold or deeded away without charge. One hundred acres were released to the federal government in 1903 to establish Fort William H. Seward.

Only one part of the original mission is still visible in Haines, a large church bell cast in Troy, New York, in 1881. Suspended in a belfry for nearly 60 years, it now hangs in front of the Presbyterian church in downtown Haines.

With arrival of Caroline and the Reverend Eugene S. Willard in the Chilkat Valley in 1881, organized missionary activity was brought to the Chilkat Tlingits. The community of Haines, named for a member of the Presbyterian Board of Home Missions, grew from the mission located near a portage between the Chilkat River and Chilkoot Inlet. (Courtesy of Sheldon Museum and Cultural Center)

Haines House, a foster home for children run by the Presbyterian Church, opened in 1921. Six years later a second building was added to increase the facility's capacity. The buildings were torn down in 1960 and a new church was built on the site. (Sheldon Museum and Cultural Center, courtesy of Elisabeth Hakkinen)

Army

Fort William H. Seward is a remnant of the great Klondike gold rush, one of several U.S. Army posts established in Alaska around the turn of the century to maintain law and order in the absence of civil government.

The first contingent of soldiers arrived in 1904. By then the gold rush had passed its peak.

A sloping grassy lawn fringed by stately wooden buildings remains as evidence that this post near Haines was created as a showcase, a symbol of the army's presence and strength.

No field work was required of troops, but a great deal of labor was devoted to beautifying the post and improving the target range. "You got out there in the boat and you'd just have to admire it," recalls George Meacock, who came as a soldier in 1927.

The Chilkat Range towers behind Fort William H. Seward, built near the turn of the century by the U.S. Army to maintain order during the gold strikes. The post, sometimes known as Chilkoot Barracks or Port Chilkoot, has had several name changes, but in the 1970s the original name was restored.
(Pete Martin, reprinted from *ALASKA GEOGRAPHIC*)

According to U.S. Army records, "a typical week's schedule generally called for drill being conducted for three-quarters of an hour daily except during target season and on days when heavy fatigue details reduced the company below one squad. Drill consisted of instruction in the new infantry drill regulations supplemented by bayonet exercise, rifle drill, calisthenics, and theoretical instructions by the company commander. Noncommissioned Officers School was held for one hour a day, three times a week."

The Thirtieth Infantry Band, one of the finest in the service, was stationed at Fort Seward in 1912 and 1913. During World War I the post had four companies of soldiers, twice the usual number, and was used for training Alaskan recruits.

Following the war many smaller army bases were decommissioned, and men who wanted to stay in Alaska were sent to Fort Seward. In 1922 the post was renamed Chilkoot Barracks to avoid postal confusion with the community of Seward on the Kenai Peninsula.

By 1925 Chilkoot Barracks was the only army post in Alaska. Both military and public interest in the territory had dwindled. The original purpose for establishing posts from Wrangell to Nome and along the Yukon River, to maintain law and order during the gold rush, had ceased to exist.

From its vantage point at the upper end of Southeast's inside passage, the post could observe pack-toting traffic bound inland over three historic trails, Chilkoot, Chilkat, and White passes. But Chilkoot Barracks had no road link with interior Alaska, and it was too far inland from the coastal perimeter of the territory to guard the shore.

When Hitler invaded Poland in 1939, Alaska's only sizable military installation had a complement of 11 officers and 286 enlisted men equipped with Springfield rifles. It had not so much as one antiaircraft gun. Its only means of transportation was a feeble 52-year-old tug, the *Fornance* (officially the *Capt. James Fornance*), which required Coast Guard rescue when she could not advance against 30-knot winds on a trip from Juneau.

The army concluded this post was never intended to repel foreign aggression.

World War II brought military activity to the Aleutian Islands, and interior and southcentral Alaska. Cadres of soldiers were transferred from Chilkoot Barracks to new installations, and the post became an induction and rest camp for military personnel.

The Alaska Highway, the first road link between Alaska and the lower states, was cut through in 1942. The following year work began on a spur that would connect Chilkoot Barracks and Haines with interior Alaska.

Early in 1946 the post was deactivated and declared surplus. The following year it was purchased by five veterans: Carl Heinmiller, Tresham Gregg, Steve Homer, James Trelford, and Martin Cordes. All but Trelford are still in Haines. They acquired 100 buildings, 400 acres, all utilities, and a road network for what later became Port Chilkoot, a second-class city. In 1970 Port Chilkoot merged with the city of Haines.

Designated a National Historic Site in 1972, the complex has once again become Fort William H. Seward. Today it combines private homes, a hotel, performing arts center, restaurant, art studios, tourism-related activities, and headquarters for Alaska Indian Arts.

The army did not totally abandon the Chilkat Valley after World War II. Development of important military installations near Fairbanks brought the need for transporting fuel. A 625-mile pipeline was completed between Haines and Fairbanks in 1955. Fuel for army and air force installations north of the Alaska Range moved through the line until 1973, when demand declined, and rail and highway transport proved more economical. A fuel storage tank farm at the terminus continues in use.

The Capt. James Fornance *played an important role in navigation on Lynn Canal in the early decades of this century. Shown here tied up with fishing boats and a seaplane in 1939, the* Fornance, *as she was commonly called, transported men and supplies from Chilkoot Barracks to other ports.* (Courtesy of Sheldon Museum and Cultural Center)

Communities

One version of an ancient Tlingit legend about the Chilkat Valley goes like this: the area was one of great movement. When the people saw what abundance of salmon, goats, moose, ducks, geese, and other resources lay all around at this particular place, they pondered what to call it. One leader stood up at a ceremonial gathering and asked, but no one responded. Then the leader said, since we came to this, "this will be forever our land." Thus it was named Klukwan.

Another interpretation for Klukwan, the only remaining Tlingit village in the Chilkat Valley, is "old and celebrated place."

No one knows how many hundreds or thousands of years ago the name might have been bestowed, but Tlingit Indians were firmly established in the Chilkat Valley long before the earliest recorded visits of white explorers.

The only surviving Tlingit village in the Chilkat Valley, Klukwan (shown here in 1895) was the center of Chilkat Indian culture and commerce. (Winter and Pond, Alaska Historical Library)

Early Presbyterian missionaries in the late 1800s wrote that "Chilkats are tallest and best-framed of all Thlinget people. They are shrewd traders. They hold most tenaciously to old-time customs."

When geographer Aurel Krause studied the Tlingits in 1879, he found the Chilkats, most powerful of all the Tlingit tribes, living in four separate villages. The principal village was Klukwan, with 65 houses and 500 to 600 inhabitants. About three miles downriver was Kathwaahltu or Klucktoo, with eight houses and a population of 125 according to the 1880 census. Kathwaahltu was destroyed in a mud slide in the 1890s; fortunately the people were away drying and smoking salmon at the time, so no lives were lost. A large

gray V still shows where the mountainside gave way.

Yendestakyeh, a village with 14 spellings for its name, was located at the mouth of the Chilkat River and in 1880 had 16 houses and 150 to 200 inhabitants. The abandoned site was largely destroyed by construction of the Haines Military Highway. It was close to the current Haines airport.

The village of Chilkat, with eight houses and about 120 people, was located on the west side of the Chilkat

Peninsula about two miles south of the center of Haines. It was abandoned around 1910.

Chilkoots, who were closely related to the Chilkats, lived in the village of Chilkoot at the head of what is now called Lutak Inlet. Most now live in Haines but retain property at Lutak.

What shattered the configuration of Tlingit culture, wrote anthropologist Frederica de Laguna, were the fur trade and Russian colonization; mining, fishing and timber industries; missionary and educational activity; and growth of white settlement. Yet, she observed in her 1949 study, the Tlingits themselves have chosen which cultural innovations to accept and how they would reinterpret them.

David Katzeek, a Juneau resident, is one of the new generation of Natives finding roles in the corporate structures created by the 1971 Alaska Native Claims Settlement Act. He lived in Klukwan intermittently until 1962 and more than 20 years later says "I don't feel I've ever actually left.

"There's a certain amount of pride for people who have roots going back to Klukwan. There's a certain amount

Assorted Chilkat blankets, hats, and masks are on display in this photo taken at Klukwan about 1900. (Winter and Pond, Alaska Historical Library)

84

of dignity and pride for the individual who comes from that community."

Despite economic difficulties, he says, Chilkat people "believe they can survive and they'll figure out a way."

Klukwan, Inc., the village corporation formed under the 1971 settlement act, owns 23,040 acres of timbered land on Long Island, 40 miles west of Ketchikan. Timber harvest has been under way since 1981 on behalf of the corporation's 235 shareholders, providing about 85 jobs at the lumber camp.

Chilkat Indian Village was formed at Klukwan under the Indian Reorganization Act of 1934 and holds 980 acres at the village site.

With a current population varying from 130 in winter to about 160 in summer, Klukwan remains self-assured, somewhat aloof, with a strong sense of identity. It endures as very much a Chilkat village.

"We like to govern ourselves," says Joe Hotch, president of Chilkat Indian Village. "We appreciate the privilege of being a sovereign community."

Clan houses retain a rich collection of artifacts. Russian guns, ceremonial artifacts, totems, and whaling guns are among the treasures in private clan ownership. Villagers have not yet chosen to display them to outsiders.

As the community of Haines enters its second century, it remains

(Above) Klukwan's population varies from about 130 in winter to about 160 in summer. (J. Schultz)

(Left) Two Klukwan fishermen carry home their salmon from the Chilkat River. (J. Schultz)

unpretentious and unassuming, without highly developed political, economic, or social structures. Some call Haines one of Alaska's best-kept secrets. A natural world of beauty is truly a few blocks away, providing a setting that coaxes forth latent artistic talents in the most unsuspecting of subjects.

The people who live here hold widely varying attitudes and opinions, but share a deep affection for the area and the life-styles it nurtures. The Chilkat Valley is a place where self-sufficiency and an overriding desire to stay are prerequisite for doing so.

With decline of the timber industry, tourism is growing in acceptance as an economic base. A luxury cruise ship is once again making Haines a port of call, after an absence of more than a dozen years. There are summer salmon bakes, demonstrations by artists, guided tours of the area, and gold rush theatrics to entice visitors.

The downtown Sheldon Museum and Cultural Center, named for pioneer resident Steve Sheldon, is

The view from 3,600-foot Mount Ripinski shows Haines (left) and Port Chilkoot facing on Portage Cove of Chilkoot Inlet and surrounded by dense forest typical of Southeast. (John Svenson)

(Above) New blends with old in the Chilkat Valley where T and S Construction tries innovative techniques to speed construction of this building. (Kurt Ramseyer)

(Left) The purple glow of winter settles over downtown Haines during the Christmas season. Winter temperatures in the valley vary with the distance from Chilkoot or Chilkat inlets. Haines's coldest record came when the thermometer dipped to minus 17° F. (Woody Bausch)

Steep mountains rise just behind Haines (population about 1,000) in this view from Portage Cove Campground. (J. Schultz)

under the loving curatorship of his daughter, Elisabeth Hakkinen. Sheldon's personal collection of artifacts formed the nucleus for the museum, which was dedicated in 1980.

Other new buildings are quietly sprouting amid the old. There is a new addition which doubles the size of the library, new medical clinic, new gallery, new swimming pool, new homes. A survey is also in progress to identify those buildings dating back to the early townsite.

Since October 1980 Haines has had its own FM radio station, Alaska Public Radio station KHNS. There are motels, variety stores, a historic hotel, restaurants, a bank, doctor, dentist, the regular amenities of small-town living.

The population of Haines has fluctuated with its economic fortunes through the years and currently hovers around 1,000 people. Much of the recent population growth has been along the outlying roads.

Lutak is a linear community of about 15 homes strung along the northeast shore of Lutak Inlet. Beyond the reach of telephone and utility lines, this is a place where neighbors help each other with the vagaries of generators, wells, and other aspects of

rural living. One of the payoffs: a front-row seat to the ever-changing panorama of sea life and weather patterns on Lutak Inlet.

Earliest residents include Raymond and Viola Carder, who started homesteading in 1956 when Carder came to Haines to work for the army tank farm. For years Carder fished to feed his family of five children. Five years ago he started fishing commercially as well.

Among the newest Lutak residents

(Above) *Haines (left) and the U.S. Army tank farm stand out along the forested shoreline of Chilkoot Inlet.* (John Mackler)

(Left) *Ray and Viola Carder, among the earliest residents of Lutak at the northeast shore of Lutak Inlet, came to the Chilkat Valley in the mid-1950s when Ray worked at the army tank farm.* (Judy Shuler)

89

are the Rev. Robert Cameron and his artist wife, Miriam, successors to the early Presbyterian missionaries who first established the town of Haines.

Chilkat Lake northwest of Haines is the valley's prime resort area. It is accessible by plane, airboat, and canoe in summer, via a snowmobile ice bridge in winter. Once it was an overnight stop on the Dalton Trail and even boasted a blacksmith shop.

Newest community in the Chilkat Valley is Mount Bether Bible Center, a few miles off the Haines Highway at Mile 26.5. About 70 people live at Mount Bether, which was established in 1975. The community owns and operates Chilkat Restaurant and Bakery in downtown Haines, Chilkat Valley General Store at Mile 27, and B and W Building Supply sawmill, also at Mile 27.

A fire destroyed their tabernacle in early December 1982 but rebuilding was soon under way. The children at Mount Bether attend a school run by the community.

At Mosquito Lake a subsistence life-style supplants traditional employment

To get away from it all, valley residents head for Chilkat Lake, three miles southwest of Klukwan and once a stop along the Dalton Trail. (Woody Bausch)

91

A cabin nestles among verdant growth of the Chilkat Valley near Mosquito Lake. Residents of about 20 to 25 households follow a subsistence life-style near the lake. (J. Schultz)

for most residents. Wood is gathered and cut for cooking and heating. Fish and game are harvested for food. The drier, sunnier climate allows gardens to flourish. Occasional odd jobs provide cash.

Some of Mosquito Lake's 20 to 25 residents live in small cabins without plumbing or electricity. Water comes from wells, roof catchment systems, or a nearby creek. People may use kerosene lamps for light, a battery operated radio for communications, a propane heater for warmth.

For city-born Chris Key, moving to Mosquito Lake in September 1982 with his wife, Lynn, was a back-to-the-roots experience.

"It's amazing what you find you can do without," he says. One of the area's appeals has been "learning how much you can do and how self-sufficient you can be."

Unlike many of their neighbors, they have a generator and well and both hold regular jobs. She is an engineer for the Alaska Marine Highway, and he is production and promotion director for KHNS-FM.

Mosquito Lake is located three and one-half miles off the Haines Highway at Mile 27. Despite the highway, natural forces can physically isolate residents. In October 1982 mud slides sent up to three feet of mud, rock, and water coursing down the road. Heavy snows the following January kept the community snowbound for several days at a stretch.

A new Mosquito Lake School on the road to the lake is doubling as community center. It opened in 1982 for grades kindergarten through four, but entire families are finding it a place to gather for companionship, for music, and for learning.

The Arts

Whether the Chilkat Valley simply attracts artists or somehow draws forth latent talents, it is a lively community for the visual and performing arts.

For the seasonally employed, arts and crafts readily convert to cottage industries which supplement other income. There are an impressive number of full-time artists and galleries.

Business offices, variety shops, and motel lobbies are likely places to look for local artwork. Fine artists are apt to have other careers as fishermen, outdoor guides, teachers, or a variety of occupations. The splendid outdoor setting, local flora and fauna, and the traditional designs of Northwest Coast Indians are recurring themes.

The sophisticated art of the Tlingit is clearly shown in the Chilkat dance blankets called *dschenu*. They are highly prized ceremonial articles, worn while intricate dances are being performed. The art of producing the traditional blankets was nearly lost but is slowly being revived. Even when Aurel Krause visited the Tlingits in 1882, he wrote that few women understood the complex weaving of these blankets which could take up to six months or more to make.

Mountain goat wool was spun by hand into yarn for the blankets. Some was dyed black, blue-green, and yellow to create the striking crest designs. The blankets were woven without looms. Warp threads were hung straight down from a round stick, the ends gathered into small bundles in animal bladder bags. Designs were copied from a pattern board. Today Chilkat blankets are valued at many thousands of dollars and are sought for public and private collections around the world.

Tlingit carving is carried on through Alaska Indian Arts, a nonprofit corporation created to revive and perpetuate Northwest Coast arts. Headquartered at Fort William H. Seward, Alaska Indian Arts was founded by Carl Heinmiller who envisioned the old army post as a center for Indian art and dance. With an education and background in primitive art, Heinmiller brought to Haines a knowledge of Tlingit art and the skills to teach it to children.

Heinmiller also formed the Chilkat Dancers in 1957. Throughout the years about 265 young Chilkats have performed with the group. They participate in ceremonies, parades, and festivals around Alaska, in the Lower 48, and overseas, and perform their traditional dances regularly for visitors in Haines. They have

performed in eight European countries, Japan, Hawaii, Washington, D.C., and in tourism promotion shows around the country.

Chilkoot dancers from Haines make up another group, the Gei-Sun Dancers. Started and led by Austin Hammond, the Gei-Sun Dancers perform each Saturday night in Haines to pass on the tradition to their young, including Hammond's grandchildren.

Peter Goll had been drawing all his life when he was attracted to Haines in 1974 by the area's incredible beauty and wealth of bird life. The

Two members of this group of Chilkat Dancers wear the highly valued Chilkat blanket; a treasure of yellow, black, and blue-green threads woven of mountain goat wool that requires many months to produce. The art of weaving these traditional blankets was nearly lost and has just recently been revived. (Janet Woodring)

following year he converted a fishing boat to a studio and took to Southeast waters. Returning to Haines in 1977, he continued to create and market black-and-white etchings of the birds that first attracted him.

Goll won a seat in the Alaska

legislature in 1982. When the rigors of campaigning forced him to lay aside art work for a time, he gained a new perspective on art. He had always enjoyed the creative process and looking at pictures, he says, but

Chilkat dancer Charles Jimmy and others, in traditional costumes, listen to speeches by elders at ceremonies honoring their old village site near Chilkoot Lake, at what is now a state campground. Below, a group of dancers entertains at the ceremony.
(Both by George Figdor)

somehow it didn't seem very important in the total scheme of the world.

"Now I find it's very wonderful to have art, to give people a place to rest their minds."

Fred ("Budge") McRae, a lifelong Haines resident, whittled to pass time in work camps during a 37-year career with state highways. Now he intercepts firewood for material to carve totems, ships, wall plaques, and figures that will be painted by his wife, Clara.

A hunk of yellow cedar that might have been chopped and burned was transformed into a full-size ram's head while McRae was recovering from a back injury. An ample block of spruce became a handsome, massive chair with an eagle for a backrest. His carvings are found in the homes of family and friends throughout the area.

Theater flourishes in Haines as well. Haines is home for Lynn Canal Community Players. Formed in 1957, it is one of the oldest continuously performing drama organizations in Alaska.

In June 1983 Haines hosted the eighth Biennial Festival of American Community Theater. Winners from nine regional festivals across the United States were invited to present the best community theater productions in the country for adjudication. The winner was invited to attend the World Festival of Amateur Theater in Japan.

Haines was named Alaska's festival city after hosting the first Alaska State Community Theater drama festival in 1973, thanks to its excellent theater facility. The Chilkat Center for the Arts provides a theater with large stage and excellent acoustics, professional lighting and sound systems, and scene shop.

The building began as a cannery in Pyramid Harbor in the late 1800s. In 1924 it was purchased by the army, dismantled, floated around Chilkat Peninsula, and reconstructed as the Education and Recreation Building at its present location on Fort William H. Seward. It suffered 20 years of disuse and neglect after the army post closed. Restoration began with the 1967 Alaska Purchase Centennial, when state and federal funds and volunteer efforts made refurbishing possible.

Studios of KHNS-FM, Haines's public radio station, have been housed in the center since 1980.

Fred McRae proudly shows off the full-size ram's head that he carved from yellow cedar while recuperating from a back injury. The chair with the eagle he carved from spruce. (Judy Shuler)

(Left) Austin Hammond holds a drum which tells the story of his people, the Chilkoots. Hammond started the Gei-Sun Dancers which carry on the culture of the Chilkoot tribe of Tlingits. (Judy Shuler)

(Below) Nurturing community theater for several years, Haines has become well known, not only for its own Lynn Canal Community Players, but also for being the site of the Alaska State Community Theater drama festival whose 1981 participants are shown here. In 1983, the city hosted the Biennial Festival of American Community Theater. (K.R. Kollodge)

95

Recreation

From climbing mountains to floating rivers to hiking gentle forest trails, the Chilkat Valley abounds with opportunities for outdoor recreation. Guide services are available for those forms demanding special equipment or savvy. Many pastimes are open to the do-it-yourself recreationists. Often, the simple pleasure of being outdoors in such a setting is quite enough.

The 6,045-acre Chilkat State Park on the Chilkat Peninsula was opened in 1978. Filled with wildflowers and wildlife, it consists of two sections. The northern unit, about 3,000 acres, includes Battery Point and Riley Summit trails.

Battery Point Trail, a gentle 2.4-mile walk along the shore, with opportunities for photography, bird watching, whale sighting, and beachcombing, can be enjoyed by hikers of any age. The last three-quarter-mile stretch follows pebble beaches and crosses Kelgaya Point, where there are wide-open vistas of

The Chilkat Peninsula entices beachcombers at low tide. After poking among the rocks, visitors can sit back and enjoy this fine view across Chilkat Inlet to the Chilkat Range.
(Raymond Frank)

Lynn Canal. Round trip from the starting point one mile east of Fort William H. Seward takes about two hours.

There are three routes to the summit of Mount Riley (1,760 feet). The steepest and most direct ascends 2.1 miles from Mud Bay Road along a marked path and takes about three and one-half hours round trip. A 3.8-mile route that begins from a road behind Fort William H. Seward and follows the city of Haines water supply access route the first two miles can be scaled on cross-country skis or snowshoes in winter. The trail takes about four and one-half hours round trip. The longest route, about five and one-half miles, begins from the Battery Point Trail on Portage Cove and is also highly recommended for snowshoes in winter. It may take as much as five hours round trip.

The southern unit of Chilkat State Park is reached about seven miles out Mud Bay Road over a winding, and at one place very steep, route that offers fine views of the Chilkat Range and Davidson and Rainbow glaciers. At the end of the road a short trail leads to a picnic shelter and beach picnic sites. The trail continues through the spruce-hemlock forest, opens into a beautiful meadow with a clear stream, then interweaves between forest and beach. The beach section should be

Chilkat State Park, 6,045 acres, offers hiking, beachcombing, picnic areas, and an abundance of natural beauty. The park's southern section affords good looks at Davidson Glacier across Chilkat Inlet.
(Michael Lee, Alaska State Park)

Linda Everett, district superintendent for southeastern Alaska, oversees Alaska State Parks holdings such as Chilkat State Park, the bald eagle preserve, and smaller waysides and historical sites, from her office in downtown Haines. (J. Schultz)

walked at low tide, as portions of the rocks along the trail may be covered or very slippery at high tide.

At various points along this trail hikers can see Eldred Rock Lighthouse, the mountains and glaciers of the Juneau Icefield, and Chilkat Islands, a group of four islands in northern Lynn Canal that look as though they might have chipped off the end of the Chilkat Peninsula and floated down the canal. Hikers may also see bears, moose, eagles, ravens, porcupines, squirrels, and rabbits.

Offshore marine life may include porpoises, seals, sea lions, killer whales, humpback whales, seabirds, and shorebirds.

There are three other state-operated campgrounds in the Chilkat Valley.

Chilkoot Lake Wayside at Mile 10 Lutak Road offers an idyllic setting of turquoise lake encircled by spectacular mountain peaks. Excellent fishing is a bonus.

Walk-in camping is the fare at Portage Cove Wayside, one-half mile past Fort William H. Seward on Beach Road. Special attraction is the expansive view of Lynn Canal with its boat traffic, and bird and marine life.

At Mosquito Lake Wayside, Mile 27 of the Haines Highway, trout rise in Mosquito Lake to lure fishermen. Campsites nestle in a quiet forest setting. Picnic shelter and boat launch are provided.

The Alaska Chilkat Bald Eagle Preserve, created in 1982, is the newest addition to the state park system in the Chilkat Valley.

In addition to the trails in Chilkat State Park, there is a spectacular trail

Eldred Rock Lighthouse lies about three miles southeast of Kataguni Island, one of the Chilkat Islands which extend into Lynn Canal from the tip of Chilkat Peninsula. The lighthouse is visible from Chilkat State Park. (Bruce Holser)

(Above) A wilderness explorer treads carefully over the ice of Le Blondeau Glacier, a four-mile river of ice which flows north out of Takhinsha Mountains to the Tsirku River Valley. (Bart Henderson)

(Right) Amid a backdrop of glaciers, rafters tackle the challenging water of the Tsirku River. Chilkat Valley rivers offer a range of rafting and kayaking experiences from quiet and serene to almost impassable. (Bart Henderson)

A steep 3.6-mile trail ascends Mount Ripinski (3,600 hundred feet). Hikers who reach the mountain's heights have an uninterrupted view of surrounding forests, towering mountains, and Lynn Canal. (Mike Smith)

(Above) *Competitors practice navigating their raft about the small-boat harbor in Haines in preparation for the Fourth of July raft race.* (George Wuerthner)

(Below) *Kathleen Flegel concentrates on winning the spoon race during Fourth of July festivities at Haines.* (Shelley Stallings)

directly above Haines. Mount Ripinski Trail takes off from the military pipeline right-of-way about one and one-quarter miles north of town. It climbs steadily through spruce-hemlock forest until the last 1,000 feet, where it ascends through open alpine meadows. Trail distance from the pipeline right-of-way to the 3,610-foot summit is 3.6 miles. Payoff for the strenuous all-day hike is an uninterrupted view of ice-topped mountains and tidal waters almost to Skagway and Juneau.

Mountain climbers too will find adventure in the Chilkat Valley. Summits rise abruptly 6,000 to 7,000 feet above sea level in the Chilkat Range, which stretches southward from the western side of Chilkat Inlet to form the eastern boundary of Glacier Bay National Park and Preserve. Along the northern boundary of Glacier Bay, the Takhinsha Mountains cradle glaciers that melt into the Tsirku and Takhin rivers. With a timberline that ends around 2,500 feet, this wild mountain area offers alpine ascents and glacier travel. Guide services are available in Haines.

Sightseeing and travel via river raft can be gentle as well as daring. Floating the braided, meandering Chilkat River is a mellow experience as the raft glides silently by eagles, an occasional bear or moose, and the always spectacular jagged peaks of the Chilkat Mountains.

Rafting on the rushing Tsirku River offers an experience beyond the beginners' level and kayaking on the upper Klehini River has been rated most difficult to impassable. River guides offer trips complete with equipment.

By winter the Alcan 200 offers a test of endurance and flexibility as snow machine drivers make the 155-mile round trip between the Alaska-British Columbia border and Dezadeash Lodge in Yukon Territory. Within one day, road rally drivers have encountered sunshine, whiteout, and bare gravel.

The contest, which has been held every year since 1969, earned its name because the first route was 200 miles long. Alcan 200 festivities also include a Calcutta auction and races on an oval track at Mile 25 on the Haines Highway. Chilkat Snowburners, the Haines snow machine club, sponsors the event around the last weekend of each January.

Canoeists seeking to duplicate John Muir's epic journey through Southeast ready their gear before departing from Haines. (Matthew Donohoe)

Gail Gilbert found her entree to winter recreation via a 100-plus-pound Mackenzie husky which used to pull her young children on a plastic sled. Deciding it would be fun for her too, Gail now uses her smaller husky and borrows another for dog sled runs to Chilkoot Lake, Chilkat Lake, toward Porcupine and into the Kelsall Valley. With the ease of travel, and the dogs for company, she feels free to go into areas where she would not normally go alone.

Other winter recreationists are discovering that cross-country skiing, eagle watching, winter picnics, and scenery that includes brilliant multi-hued ice falls colored by mineralized water combine to create an experience unmatched anywhere.

———————————

Despite economic uncertainties, many valley residents do not want major, rapid change. If change must come, they'll opt for slow doses.

Meanwhile, they dwell amid great beauty and natural wealth. There is wood for the stove, fish for the table, and perhaps even moose and goat. People can live simply here, and pretty much as they see fit.

Haines publisher and longtime resident Ray Menaker recalls when the board of directors for the Alaska Visitors Association met in Haines. It was February 1977. One lumber mill had just been sold, the other was closed. The previous summer, commercial fishermen had waited out a seven-week closing before the season opened. There was no real employment in the valley.

The new visitors association director, a newcomer to the state, inquired eagerly about Haines's major industry.

Menaker responded, "Worry."

Then lifelong resident Elisabeth Hakkinen spoke. She could remember three or four times when there was no money in town. None. Then something would come along.

"I think people like to live here," she reflected, "and they find a way to do it."

104

Alaska Geographic® Back Issues

The North Slope, Vol. 1, No. 1. The charter issue of *ALASKA GEOGRAPHIC*® took a long, hard look at the North Slope and the then-new petroleum development at "the top of the world." *Out of print.*

One Man's Wilderness, Vol. 1, No. 2. The story of a dream shared by many, fulfilled by a few; a man goes into the Bush, builds a cabin and shares his incredible wilderness experience. Color photos. 116 pages, $9.95.

Admiralty . . . Island in Contention, Vol. 1, No. 3. An intimate and multifaceted view of Admiralty: its geological and historical past, its present-day geography, wildlife and sparse human population. Color photos. 78 pages, $5.00

Fisheries of the North Pacific: History, Species, Gear & Processes, Vol. 1, No. 4. The title says it all. This volume is out of print, but the book, from which it was excerpted, is available in a revised, expanded large-format volume. 424 pages. $24.95.

The Alaska-Yukon Wild Flowers Guide, Vol. 2, No. 1. First Northland flower book with both large, color photos and detailed drawings of every species described. Features 160 species, common and scientific names and growing height. Vertical-format book edition now available. 218 pages, $12.95.

Richard Harrington's Yukon, Vol. 2, No. 2. The Canadian province with the colorful past *and* present. *Out of print.*

Prince William Sound, Vol. 2, No. 3. This volume explores the people and resources of the Sound. *Out of print.*

Yakutat: The Turbulent Crescent, Vol. 2, No. 4. History, geography, people — and the impact of the coming of the oil industry. *Out of print.*

Glacier Bay: Old Ice, New Land, Vol. 3, No. 1. The expansive wilderness of southeastern Alaska's Glacier Bay National Monument (recently proclaimed a national park and preserve) unfolds in crisp text and color photographs. Records the flora and fauna of the area, its natural history, with hike and cruise information, plus a large-scale color map. 132 pages, $11.95.

The Land: Eye of the Storm, Vol. 3, No. 2. The future of one of the earth's biggest pieces of real estate! *This volume is out of print,* but the latest on the Alaska lands controversy is detailed completely in Volume 8, Number 4.

Richard Harrington's Antarctic, Vol. 3, No. 3. The Canadian photojournalist guides readers through remote and little understood regions of the Antarctic and Subantarctic. More than 200 color photos and a large fold-out map. 104 pages, $8.95

The Silver Years of the Alaska Canned Salmon Industry: An Album of Historical Photos, Vol. 3, No. 4. The grand and glorious past of the Alaska canned salmon industry. *Out of print.*

Alaska's Volcanoes: Northern Link in the Ring of Fire, Vol. 4, No. 1. Scientific overview supplemented with eyewitness accounts of Alaska's historic volcano eruptions. Includes color and black-and-white photos and a schematic description of the effects of plate movement upon volcanic activity. 88 pages. *Temporarily out of print.*

The Brooks Range: Environmental Watershed, Vol. 4, No. 2. An impressive work on a truly impressive piece of Alaska — The Brooks Range. *Out of print.*

Kodiak: Island of Change, Vol. 4, No. 3. Russians, wildlife, logging and even petroleum . . . an island where change is one of the few constants. *Out of print.*

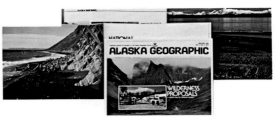

Wilderness Proposals: Which Way for Alaska's Lands? Vol. 4, No. 4. This volume gives yet another detailed analysis of the many Alaska lands questions. *Out of print.*

Cook Inlet Country, Vol. 5, No. 1. Our first comprehensive look at the area. A visual tour of the region — its communities, big and small, and its countryside. Begins at the southern tip of the Kenai Peninsula, circles Turnagain Arm and Knik Arm for a close-up view of Anchorage, and visits the Matanuska and Susitna valleys and the wild, west side of the inlet. *Out of print.*

Southeast: Alaska's Panhandle, Vol. 5, No. 2. Explores southeastern Alaska's maze of fjords and islands, mossy forests and glacier-draped mountains — from Dixon Entrance to Icy Bay, including all of the state's fabled Inside Passage. Along the way are profiles of every town, together with a look at the region's history, economy, people, attractions and future. Includes large fold-out map and seven area maps. 192 pages, $12.95.

Bristol Bay Basin, Vol. 5, No. 3. Explores the land and the people of the region known to many as the commercial salmon-fishing capital of Alaska. Illustrated with contemporary color and historic black-and-white photos. Includes a large fold-out map of the region. *Out of print.*

The Aurora Borealis, Vol. 6, No. 2. Here one of the world's leading experts — Dr. S.-I. Akasofu of the University of Alaska — explains in an easily understood manner, aided by many diagrams and spectacular color and black-and-white photos, what causes the aurora, how it works, how and why scientists are studying it today and its implications for our future. 96 pages, $7.95.

Alaska's Great Interior, Vol. 7, No. 1. Alaska's rich Interior country, west from the Alaska-Yukon Territory border and including the huge drainage between the Alaska Range and the Brooks Range, is covered thoroughly. Included are the region's people, communities, history, economy, wilderness areas and wildlife. Illustrated with contemporary color and black-and-white photos. Includes a large fold-out map. 128 pages, $9.95.

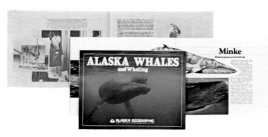

Alaska Whales and Whaling, Vol. 5, No. 4. The wonders of whales in Alaska — their life cycles, travels and travails — are examined, with an authoritative history of commercial and subsistence whaling in the North. Includes a fold-out poster of 14 major whale species in Alaska in perspective, color photos and illustrations, with historical photos and line drawings. 144 pages, $12.95.

Alaska's Native People, Vol. 6, No. 3. In this edition the editors examine the varied worlds of the Inupiat Eskimo, Yup'ik Eskimo, Athabascan, Aleut, Tlingit, Haida and Tsimshian. Included are sensitive, informative articles by Native writers, plus a large, four-color map detailing the Native villages and defining the language areas. 304 pages, $24.95.

A Photographic Geography of Alaska, Vol. 7, No. 2. An overview of the entire state — a visual tour through the six regions of Alaska: Southeast, Southcentral/Gulf Coast, Alaska Peninsula and Aleutians, Bering Sea Coast, Arctic and Interior. Plus a handy appendix of valuable information — "Facts About Alaska." Approximately 160 color and black-and-white photos and 35 maps. 192 pages. Revised in 1983. $15.95.

Yukon-Kuskokwim Delta, Vol. 6, No. 1. This volume explores the people and life-styles of one of the most remote areas of the 49th state. *Out of print.*

The Stikine, Vol. 6, No. 4. River route to three Canadian gold strikes in the 1800s. This edition explores 400 miles of Stikine wilderness, recounts the river's paddle-wheel past and looks into the future. Illustrated with contemporary color photos and historic black-and-white; includes a large fold-out map. 96 pages, $9.95.

The Aleutians, Vol. 7, No. 3. Home of the Aleut, a tremendous wildlife spectacle, a major World War II battleground and now the heart of a thriving new commercial fishing industry. Contemporary color and black-and-white photographs, and a large fold-out map. 224 pages, $14.95.

Alaska Mammals, Vol. 8, No. 2. From tiny ground squirrels to the powerful polar bear, and from the tundra hare to the magnificent whales inhabiting Alaska's waters, this volume includes 80 species of mammals found in Alaska. Included are beautiful color photographs and personal accounts of wildlife encounters. 184 pages, $12.95.

Alaska's Glaciers, Vol. 9, No. 1. Examines in-depth the massive rivers of ice, their composition, exploration, present-day distribution and scientific significance. Illustrated with many contemporary color and historical black-and-white photos, the text includes separate discussions of more than a dozen glacial regions. 144 pages, $9.95.

Klondike Lost: A Decade of Photographs by Kinsey & Kinsey, Vol. 7, No. 4. An album of rare photographs and all-new text about the lost Klondike boomtown of Grand Forks, second in size only to Dawson during the gold rush. Introduction by noted historian Pierre Berton: 138 pages, area maps and more than 100 historical photos, most never before published. $12.95.

The Kotzebue Basin, Vol. 8, No. 3. Examines northwestern Alaska's thriving trading area of Kotzebue Sound and the Kobuk and Noatak river basins. Contemporary color and historical black-and-white photographs. 184 pages, $12.95.

Sitka and Its Ocean/Island World, Vol. 9, No. 2. From the elegant capital of Russian America to a beautiful but modern port, Sitka, on Baranof Island, has become a commercial and cultural center for southeastern Alaska. Pat Roppel, longtime Southeast resident and expert on the region's history, examines in detail the past and present of Sitka, Baranof Island, and neighboring Chichagof Island. Illustrated with contemporary color and historical black-and-white photographs. 128 pages, $9.95.

Wrangell-Saint Elias, Vol. 8, No. 1. Mountains, including the continent's second- and fourth-highest peaks, dominate this international wilderness that sweeps from the Wrangell Mountains in Alaska to the southern Saint Elias range in Canada. Illustrated with contemporary color and historical black-and-white photographs. Includes a large fold-out map. 144 pages, $9.95.

Alaska National Interest Lands, Vol. 8, No. 4. Following passage of the bill formalizing Alaska's national interest land selections (d-2 lands), longtime Alaskans Celia Hunter and Ginny Wood review each selection, outlining location, size, access, and briefly describing the region's special attractions. Illustrated with contemporary color photographs. 242 pages, $14.95.

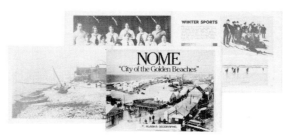

Islands of the Seals: The Pribilofs, Vol. 9, No. 3.
Great herds of northern fur seals drew Russians and Aleuts to these remote Bering Sea islands where they founded permanent communities and established a unique international commerce. Illustrated with contemporary color and historical black-and-white photographs. 128 pages, $9.95.

ANCHORAGE and the Cook Inlet Basin . . . Alaska's Commercial Heartland, Vol. 10, No. 2.
An update of what's going on in "Anchorage country" . . . the Kenai, the Susitna Valley, and Matanuska. Heavily illustrated in color and including three illustrated maps . . . one an uproarious artist's forecast of "Anchorage 2035." 168 pages, $14.95.

Nome: City of the Golden Beaches, Vol. 11, No. 1. The colorful history of Alaska's most famous gold rush town has never been told like this before. With a text written by Terrence Cole, and illustrated with hundreds of rare black-and-white photos, the book traces the story of Nome from the crazy days of the 1900 gold rush. 184 pages, $14.95.

Alaska's Oil/Gas & Minerals Industry, Vol. 9, No. 4. Experts detail the geological processes and resulting mineral and fossil fuel resources that are now in the forefront of Alaska's economy. Illustrated with historical black-and-white and contemporary color photographs. 216 pages, $12.95.

Alaska's Salmon Fisheries, Vol. 10, No. 3. The work of *ALASKA®* magazine outdoors editor Jim Rearden, this issue takes a comprehensive look at Alaska's most valuable commercial fishery. Through text and photos, readers will learn about the five species of salmon caught in Alaska, different types of fishing gear and how each works, and will take a district-by-district tour of salmon fisheries throughout the state. 128 pages, $12.95.

Alaska's Farms and Gardens, Vol. 11, No. 2. An overview of the past, present, and future of agriculture in Alaska, and a wealth of information on how to grow your own fruit and vegetables in the north. 144 pages, $12.95.

All prices U.S. funds.

NEXT ISSUE:
The Northwest Territories, Vol. 11, No. 4.
This issue takes an in-depth look at Canada's immense Northwest Territories, which comprises some of the most beautiful and isolated land in North America. Supervising editor Richard Harrington has brought together informative text and color photos covering such topics as geology and mineral resources, prehistoric people, native art, and the search for the Northwest Passage. Also included is a look under the ice of the Canadian Arctic. To members in November 1984. Price to be announced.

Adventure Roads North: The Story of the Alaska Highway and Other Roads in *The MILEPOST®*, Vol. 10, No. 1. From Alaska's first highway — the Richardson — to the famous Alaska Highway, first overland route to the 49th state, text and photos provide a history of Alaska's roads and take a mile-by-mile look at the country they cross. 224 pages, $14.95.

Koyukuk Country, Vol. 10, No. 4. This issue explores the vast drainage of the Koyukuk River, third largest in Alaska. Text and photos provide information on the land and offer insights into the life-style of the people who live and have lived along the Koyukuk. 152 pages, $14.95.

The Alaska Geographic Society

Box 4-EEE, Anchorage, AK 99509

Membership in The Alaska Geographic Society is $30 (U.S. funds), which includes the following year's four quarterlies which explore a wide variety of subjects in the Northland, each issue an adventure in great photos, maps, and excellent research. Members receive their quarterlies as part of the membership fee at considerable savings over the prices which nonmenbers must pay for individual book editions.

ALASKA EARTHLINES/TIDELINES — an eight-times-a-year newsprint magazine published by The Alaska Geographic Society — deals with a variety of natural resource subjects for classroom study. A new volume begins in September and ends in May. (December/January is a combined issue.) **Student subscriptions** generally include the 8 issues published during a school year. **Single subscriptions** begin with the current issue and continue until 8 consecutive issues have been sent. Subscription prices:

STUDENT: $1.50 per subscription: minimum order, 10 subscriptions sent to one address.

SINGLE: $3.50 per subscription. (Payments to be made in U.S. funds.)

A SAMPLE COPY can be yours for $1.00, postpaid. Make checks payable to The Alaska Geographic Society, and send with your order to *Alaska Earthlines/Tidelines*, Box 4-EEE, Anchorage, Alaska 99509. Your canceled check is your receipt. **GIFT SUBSCRIPTIONS** will be announced to the recipient with a card signed in your name.